THE FIVE SUPREME SECRETS OF LIFE

THE FIVE SUPREME SECRETS OF LIFE

Unveiling the Ways to Attain Wealth, Love and God

Sirshree

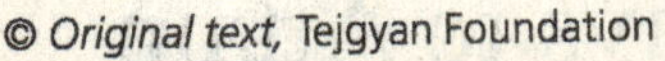

First published 2008
Reprinted 2010, 2012, 2018

ISBN 978-81-8328-121-8

Published by
Wisdom Tree
4779/23 Ansari Road
Darya Ganj, New Delhi-110002
Ph.: 011-23247966/67/68
wisdomtreebooks@gmail.com

Printed in India

CONTENTS

Preface

When Newton discovered the secret of the law of gravity, the entire face of science took a new turn. The subsequent inventions and technological developments in the material world literally changed the style of life for humans. Today there is no invention or innovation that does not use the law of gravity. If due to the principle of gravity such drastic changes in human life could be brought about, then can you imagine what would happen if the secret laws that govern our life were to come out in the open? Such a possibility now lies in your hands, as you will discover on reading this book.

Why is it that men consult palmists? It is because they want to know the secret of what tomorrow holds for them. By knowing the secret of the future, they want to be happy in the present. They believe that if in the future all problems were to dissolve, they would live peacefully in the present. That is why people run after fortune-tellers, hoping to learn about their future. But can the fortune-teller predict everyone's future to be bright and successful? No. Everybody's future can never be similar and neither is it possible to be rid of one's problems by learning about one's future. For finding relief from problems, one needs to know the secrets of the present. On knowing the secrets of the present, one can be happy. The secret of the present is not imaginary, but real, while the secret of the future is imaginary and incomplete. Even the greatest of astrologers admit that all their predictions can never come true and agree that many times they have been proved wrong. Hence, not getting entangled with the secrets of the future, learn the supreme secrets of life that will improve your present. These secrets are the laws of a supreme life; they tell us about the present. They have nothing to do with the future. So, come, let us break free from the cycle of fate and fortune.

What would your reaction be if you could clearly see that the problems you are facing in life are actually no problems at all? The truth is that every problem brings either a solution with it, or a gift for you, or a ladder for your progress, or a lesson you need to learn, or a challenge that you need to overcome so as to emerge stronger. As this first supreme secret of life unfolds in the first part of the book, the perspective (the truth perspective) will become apparent. When you imbibe this secret, your problems will dissolve automatically.

The second supreme secret of life is presented in the second part of the book. This secret teaches the importance of living in the present and how to live so. But that is not all; this secret teaches you the greatest meditation that will take you towards attaining God which is the true purpose of human life. Attention on attention is the greatest meditation. This secret will help you train your attention. The importance of training one's attention can be understood through the following analogy.

A village-woman was carrying a pot of water on her head. Her child, holding on to her hand, was accompanying her. They were returning home. You must have seen such a scene quite often in villages or in movies or paintings. Now view this scene from a different perspective. This new perspective presents the second supreme secret of life.

Home was the destination for the woman. Guiding her child, she was walking towards her home. Along with this, her attention was constantly on her pot. How was this possible? This was possible because she had trained herself to focus her attention through strong resolve and regular practice.

Similarly with us, our destination (home) is the sole purpose of our life (the secret of life). The daily chores of our life constitute our children. The pot kept on the head is our centre, our source, our *tejasthan*. We too have to learn to walk like this woman. This does not mean that we have to copy her style of walking. It means that while working, we too must focus our attention on our centre. In the process, many a times our attention tends to slip away from the centre; yet we have to forcefully bring our attention back again and again. This is possible only with regular practice and a thirst for the truth.

Who is truly rich? By rich it does not mean having an ample amount of money. Life has already proved this to us. Our bank holds only one-fourth of our wealth. We can attain the seemingly impossible combination of time, money, attention and love in abundance. This is what constitutes all the wealth that one can attain in this world. The third supreme secret is the secret of prosperity and progress in its true and fullest sense. The one who grasps this secret, in whatever position he is today, can easily attain this prosperity. It is not the amount but the right balance of all these four that he gives to others and retains for himself that determines his true wealth. This secret of how to grow prosperous in every way constitutes the third part of the book. You will also realise that this prosperity is essential to fulfil our true purpose of life.

Suppose a difficult situation appears in your life. Your first reaction is that of incredulity, 'Why had this to happen to me alone?' But as time passes and so does the situation, you are found saying, 'It was good that such a situation came into my life. Only because of it, I have grown stronger and achieved a lot in my life today.' However, when the next tough situation arises your reaction is the same again — that of incredulity. Why is it so? What is the perspective that you are missing? What is it you cannot see during a situation that disturbs your balance? Why is it that you grow wise to a situation only after it has passed. It is this perspective that constitutes the fourth supreme secret of life. This extremely powerful secret will bring balance and stability, knowing that whatever is happening now is exactly what is needed for your progress according to the larger picture. You will realise the secret behind the statement, 'Every scene is a preparation for the next scene.'

The first four secrets are essentials to maintain your focus on the true purpose of life. It is the fifth that is the grand finale that comprises the true purpose — that of knowing who you truly are. What would you call a lion that thinks it is a lamb and does not want to know the truth, even if it were possible to do so? Such a lion will probably attain the highest that is possible in the domain of the sheep and pass away in pride of its achievement, but ignorant of its true possibilities. What is an achievement for it after a lot of struggle is actually a negligible fraction for its true nature. Each one is a lion, but you consider yourself to be a sheep. Everyone has infinite possibilities. For these possibilities to manifest, it is essential to know who you really are. You can try to attain only that goal, that possibility, which is visible to you. All limitations lie in the misconception that he himself is the body. The limitations of the body become our limitations. The fifth supreme secret is the end of this misconception and the beginning of the opening up of the true possibilities of human birth.

These five supreme secrets encompass the entire secrets of life. On imbibing these five secrets, you can derive happiness from within yourself whenever you want and as much as you want.

Through this book, imbibe the secrets so that you can fulfil the highest purpose of your life.

INTRODUCTION

Chapter One

The Vision of Supreme Life

Life Without Death

Welcome to all the lovers of truth who wish to seek the truth and the supreme secrets of life. Happy thoughts to all of you. Happy thoughts are those thoughts, which liberate you from false beliefs. Happy thoughts explain the final knowledge of the truth. Happy thoughts are desires, which liberate you from the discourse of desire before vanishing. Happy thoughts show you the vision of supreme life.

Is life a journey, which everyone has to endure? Is life a path, which everyone has to walk, suffering jolts and jerks? Has no one known or understood the true meaning of life? Is life nothing but just moving on, where one needs to simply go on day and night? Is life a struggle where the battle of success and failure is constantly fought? Is life a riddle that sometimes makes you laugh and sometimes makes you cry? Is life an ice-cream which needs to be eaten while there is still time? Is life a bird trapped in the cage of death? Is life truly experienced only in the abode of the poor? Or can life become liberated from death?

There is life in every human being. Life itself is consciousness. Life is the name of being, open and giving. Life is that magic in whose presence the nightingale sings songs, the butterfly tastes nectar, the flowers spread fragrance, the clouds shower rains, the poet composes poetry and the devotee sings hymns. Life is a one-handed clap as there is nothing else in the universe other than life. When life experiences life through the body of man, the one-handed clap is experienced — that which has been called *anhad naadh*, the infinite note. Life is that consciousness which from being a witness to the world wants to be a self-witness.

For life to express itself and manifest its colours, its forms and its qualities, what does it need? For life to fully express itself, it needs a human body, which is free from beliefs; a body that is free of tendencies, bad habits and patterns; a body that is free from lethargy. For life to open up all its dimensions, a human body is needed that is filled with divine devotion and love and is free from hatred, jealousy, malice and ego. In order to attain such a body, one has to make life a *sadhana*, a spiritual practice. Instead of tormenting one's own or another's body, one should train it to sit in meditation. Understand this through an example.

There was a washerman who visited the river daily to wash clothes. He would take his donkey along with him. He also had a goat and a monkey at home. Every day he tied up his goat and monkey before leaving home. As soon as the washerman left, the monkey would open the rope, jump up and roam around. Then just before the master returned, the monkey would tie itself up again and sit quietly.

One day the washerman brought a bagful of peanuts and kept it in his hut before leaving for work. The monkey, as usual, untied itself and ate up all the peanuts. It tied itself up again. But before tying itself, it untied the rope of the goat. Now you can imagine what would have happened! The washerman returned home and saw the empty bag of peanuts and the untied rope of the goat. Angered beyond control, he severely thrashed the goat. The monkey sat silently, enjoying the scene and feeling happy. Just see, the goat got beaten up for no fault of its own.

In this story, who is the goat? Who is the monkey? What are

the peanuts? Who is the washerman? The goat in the story symbolises our body, which gets beaten up. The monkey represents the restless mind, which keeps jumping around. No sooner does an incident occur than the mind begins with its commentary: "What happened was good or bad... why did this happen... it should not have happened... it would have been better if it had happened the other way... it would have been good if this had not happened..." and so on. How the mind jumps around! Hence it is said that when the mind is turned inwards, it becomes a temple. If the mind is turned outwards, it becomes a monkey. The temple you see outside was created to indicate and remind you of this very fact. On seeing the temple, you should remember to notice if your mind ever goes within or is it always engrossed outside in the attractions of *maya*, the external illusory world.

With the help of the above example, let us try to understand whose fault it actually is and who gets punished for it. Man begins the journey towards the supreme life, thinking that 'if I observe this fast, my mind will calm down and become serene. Then I will know the supreme truth.' Thinking thus, some continue to fast. Others perform penance and austerities and torment the body. Some wake up at 4 a.m. in the morning and take a dip in the Ganges, the holy river. Thinking that on a particular day one should not eat certain things or that it is inauspicious to do something or go to a particular place on such and such day, man accumulates plenty of fears.

You may have read or heard or followed religiously rituals associated with the body. But, if you want to attain supreme life, you need to know that tormenting the body is wrong. Understanding and training should be given to the mind.

Many paths have been put forth before us, such as chanting, penance, rituals, *mantras*, *seva* (service), religion, *karma* (deeds) and meditation. But on following these paths, if the truth does not emerge, the body keeps getting beaten up. Understand the supreme secrets of life to allow the expression of life to occur through you. If that happens, life becomes a supreme life.

If we drink tea just after eating a sweet, what happens? The tea tastes insipid as the taste of the sweet lingers on the tongue, overpowering the taste of tea. In the same manner, if we have any preconceived opinions or beliefs, then we need to read this book after keeping our beliefs aside for a while. Only then will we be able to understand these secrets and principles of life.

On learning the secrets of life, there can never be lack of joy in life. Due to the absence of knowledge, we tend to derive happiness from all the wrong sources. Some consume alcohol, some indulge in gambling, some go to the racecourse, some say, 'I want to attain this… I want to possess that… I should get a raise in my salary…' so as to derive happiness. They do not know that true happiness lies within us and all we need to know is how to attain it.

Once we know the secrets of life, we will never feel the lack of joy, nor will there ever be a dearth of whatever we want in life. We will stop being dependent on others or looking for praise from others. We will stop saying, "Someone should praise me. Someone should do the work that I want done. Someone should bring me a gift on my birthday, so that I can be happy. Someone else must do something for me, only then will I attain happiness." But, is it not possible that happiness lies within me? I can derive it whenever I want and as much as I want. Have you ever met a person who says, "I am happy because I am. This is enough for me. My being itself is the cause of happiness."

It is a happy person who can transform his life from life to a supreme life. Only a happy person can witness a true life, which cannot be seen through the eyes but only felt through the heart.

When life experiences life through the body of man, then the one-handed clap, the *anhad naadh* (the infinite note) occurs.

Chapter Two

House of the Supreme

You are Guests on Earth

Every human being on this Earth is a guest. If everyone is a guest, then the question arises, 'Whose guests are we?'

We are all guests of the Supreme. If we *visualise* the House of the Supreme Being, then our presence, our thinking, our mannerisms, our behaviour will change. When we visit someone's house as a guest, how long do we stay there? While staying there, do we think that the room given to us is ours and no one should enter? We do not show this obstinacy in another's house because we are conscious that the house is not ours and that we are guests. Similarly we are guests of the Supreme Being and if we fully realise this, our conduct would undergo a radical change from what it is today.

If there is some useful equipment in a person's house and the person does not know of its existence, he is unable to make its use. For example, a person has an umbrella at home but he does not know about it. He thus has to bear the heat of the sun or get wet in the rain. Then someone points out to him, "You have an umbrella and it is in your own house."

After coming to know that he has an umbrella, if he is merely happy about it but does not use it, the purpose is defeated. Until someone teaches him to open the umbrella and use it, he continues to suffer the heat and rain.

Ten people from a village decided to go to a particular place. Knowing that they were all dim-witted, their friends instructed them, "Ten of you are going. See to it that all ten of you return."

On the way, they had to cross a river, so they swam across it. After reaching the other side, they decided to first count how many of them had managed to cross over. One among them began to count and ended up counting nine persons. Thinking that only nine out of ten had crossed the river, he began to cry. He thought that one of them had drowned in the river. You must have realised by now that he had counted everyone in the group except himself.

Man too does the same in life. He counts everyone except himself. If you were to ask a person, 'Do you know your true self?', his head would drop in shame as he has time to spend on finding about everyone else but himself. He knows all the answers about the world. If he were to enter a contest on general knowledge, he can win and become a millionaire, but if you were to ask him, 'Who are you?', he would be left speechless.

It is the same with the five supreme secrets of life. Man has known these secrets since the very beginning. We are being told here what we already know. The five secrets are such that everybody knows them, yet we have to be told because we do not know them in words and nor do we know how to use them.

Through this book we can learn how to use the supreme secrets of life. Along with this, we will learn about a house in which we will see many different things. This house is the House of the Supreme (*see* illustration).

When we enter the House of the Supreme, we find that the floor is made of black and white tiles, just like a chessboard. When we enter this house, we have to walk across these black and white tiles. These tiles symbolise the joys and sorrows of life. When we walk across the floor, it indicates moving ahead through these joys and sorrows. If we understand why we have come to the House of the Supreme (the Earth), then this house becomes an opportunity for

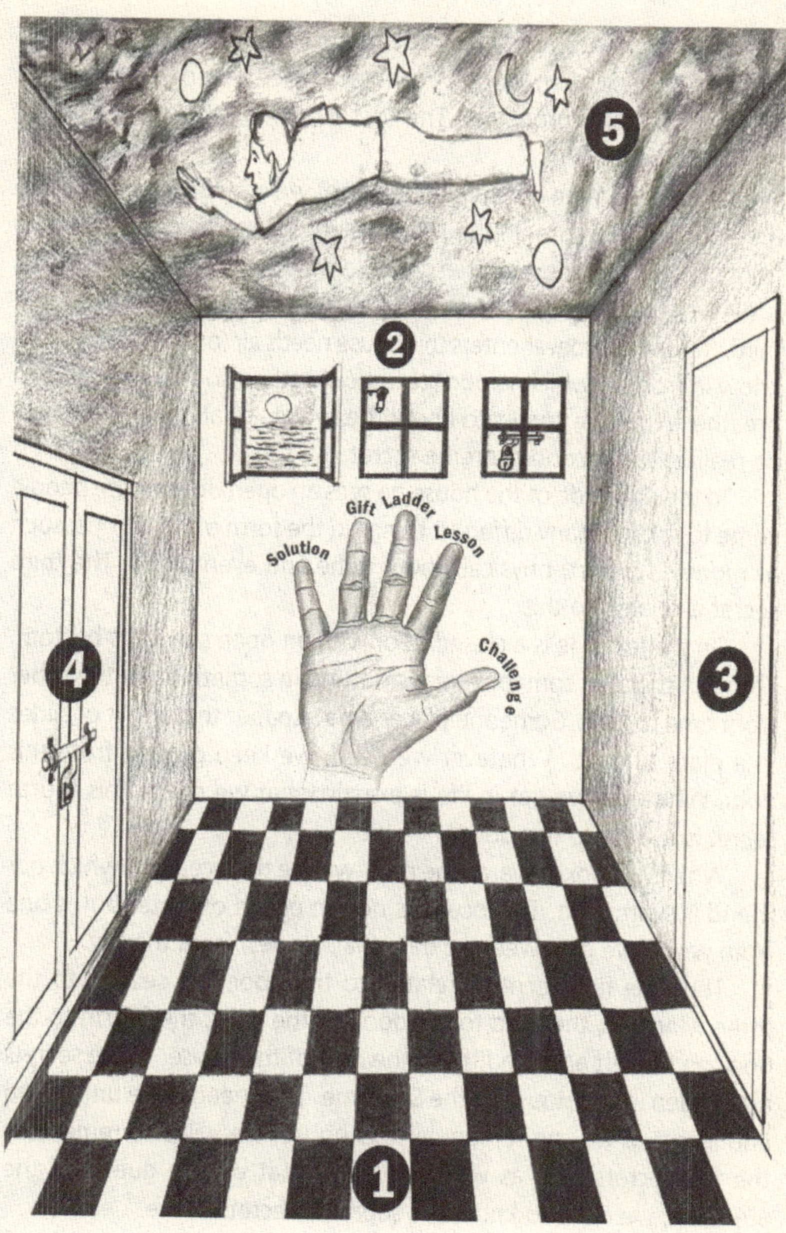

The House of the Supreme containing the five supreme secrets of life

self-expression — a cause for joy. If we are not aware of everything about this house, then incidents that take place here become a cause of difficulties and problems. The first supreme secret is related to these problems.

On entering the house, the first sight we encounter is related to the floor of the house. In the second sight we see three windows in front of us. Something is written on these windows. On the first window is written the word 'past', on the second it is 'present' and on the third, 'future'. Whoever enters this house needs air (oxygen). He should know in front of which window he should stand so that he is able to breathe. When he comes to know the secrets of all three windows, he realises the second supreme secret.

To the right side of the house he sees an open door where people come to ask for many different things in the form of donations, such as money, support, physical labour, time and even blood. The third secret is related to this.

On the left side is a closed door with an open slot at its bottom. Through that slot someone keeps putting in something or the other from time to time. Someone places a newspaper through it or slides in a plate of food. Whatever we need, we keep getting from this door. Whatever we get in life is exactly what we need. This fourth secret is related to this door.

When we look towards the roof, we see the ocean, in which our friend is swimming. This ocean is not an ocean of water but is one from which we get sweet ice balls (hail-stones) from the sky.

Thus the first secret is related to the floor, the second to the three windows, the third to the door on the right, the fourth to the door on the left and the fifth to the roof of the house. These secrets are hidden in the House of the Supreme. They need to be unravelled and learnt. If we can remember this house, we will also remember the five secrets. Just as we have learnt that we are guests of the Supreme, we need to know the supreme secrets of life.

Chapter Three

Is Becoming a Millionaire the Goal of Man?

Obtain Real Wealth

The aim of man's life is not merely to fill his stomach or empty it, or read the newspaper, or study in school and college, get married, give birth to children, become a mother or father-in-law and a grandparent. Life is not limited just to these things.

Only by becoming life can we really know what life truly is. We do not have to live life; we have to become life. When we read such lines or such secrets in words for the first time, we may not grasp their meaning. But once we understand these secrets with the help of the examples that follow, then we will be forced to admit, 'Indeed! It is so.'

Set the highest goal to give direction to life

We need to set the highest goal for ourselves and try to achieve it. 'As will be our goal, so will things begin to get organised for us' and 'the higher the goal we set for ourselves, the greater is the strength that Nature endows us with' — these are the laws of Nature. Those who understand these will never aim small. If we want to experience the power of Nature within us, then we need to set the highest goal. An aim in life gives direction to our mind, body and intellect. How many people manage to set a goal for themselves? Among them, how many sit down to write it? How many set the highest goal? How many have faith in achieving that highest goal? Set the highest goal for yourself today itself. It should be such a goal that just the sound of it makes you excited, joyous and inspired to work towards achieving it, while erasing all apprehensions. Write down this goal not only in your diary but also on chits of paper and paste them where your eyes can see them as often as possible. For instance, paste it on the mirror, the computer, the refrigerator, your hairbrush, your key chain, etc. If you do not wish to reveal it to others, then write it in code language. Contemplate on it day in and day out.

Take the case of an infant who is unable to walk as yet. He needs to learn to walk because he is destined to become a mountain climber. What should we do to make him walk? We will tell him, "There are two pits and a ball in front of you. If you throw the ball into one of the pits, you will get a toffee. If you fetch the ball from one pit and throw it into the other, you will get another toffee. If you do this twenty times within half an hour, you will get a big chocolate."

Hearing this, the child becomes happy as he has a new game to play now. Throwing the ball from one pit to the other, he learns to walk in the process. Earlier when he tried to walk without this game, his attention was concentrated only on his legs. When attention is focused entirely on the legs, then the chances of falling are more. When someone goes on the stage and constantly wonders if he is speaking correctly, things are bound to go wrong. But when the child's attention is on the ball, he learns to walk easily, while moving towards the ball. Soon the child begins to enjoy the game so much that he keeps on playing with the ball all the time, even after he has learnt to walk perfectly. The child forgets that he had to climb the mountain — the true purpose of his life.

Similarly, we begin to play the worldly game to learn something from it so that we may apply the learning for achieving our ultimate purpose. This prime aim gets sidelined, as we get caught in this game.

If we keep worrying about profit and loss, the purpose for which we have come into this world will never be fulfilled. Here, at such times, our guru reminds use of our folly by asking, "Is this why you came to Earth?"

It is not that we need to relinquish the world, but we have to see how we can fulfil our true purpose even while engaging in worldly matters. Once we grasp this point, we will learn to focus on the truth and begin to work on our inner progress. If we were to constantly think only about money, there would be no progress and we will be running after money all the time.

Contemplate on the five supreme secrets of life for thirteen days. When we sincerely contemplate on all the five secrets for thirteen days, they get easily assimilated. Hence, ask yourself daily, 'In the series of events that are taking place today, which of the secrets should I work on? Should I work on the floor, the three windows, the right door, the left door or the roof?' On the basis of the answers to the questions, decide on the action to take. You will learn something through that action. When you apply this learning to other situations, you discover that supreme life has become your very nature. This understanding will remain with you forever. In this manner, by working on each of the secrets, you can move ahead.

We were told to work on these secrets for thirteen days and no more or no less because we need to free ourselves from all kinds of false beliefs. Some people consider thirteen to be an unlucky number. The flickering of an eye, the itching of the palm, a cat crossing one's path, and many more such incidents carry beliefs with them which need to be dispelled. Hence, we have been given thirteen days to work on the secrets as it would also help us get over such superstitious beliefs. After working on these secrets for thirteen days, we will be able to assimilate them forever. These secrets are irrefutable, unbreakable, eternal and complete. We need to work on these secrets while trying to maintain faith. Is it that man has to attain only one kind of wealth? No, it is not so. Many kinds of wealth have been created for man. On understanding these secrets we can attain different kinds of wealth — the wealth of love, the fortune of meditation and the treasure of time and health.

It would be wrong to assume that one can be happy only when the size of one's house or bank balance increases. If this were so, the world today would not be filled with millions of unhappy millionaires. On talking to such millionaires, we find that despite having all kinds of pleasures, comforts and money, there is no dearth of misery in their life. If by attaining enough wealth (money), happiness could be attained, then these people should have been the happiest in the world. But this is not so. We keep reading about their family problems in newspapers or seeing them on the television. We find negative things in their life too. Hence this should prove to us that to attain true wealth, we must understand the first secret, provided we are willing to remove the blinkers of false beliefs covering our eyes. By blinkers of beliefs is meant that we look at things based on our beliefs, and that distorts our perception of reality. We need to look at everything with a fresh perspective.

For example, a person asks his friend, "When our head aches, we say we suffer from a headache. What would we say, if our neck pains?"

The friend replies, "Pain in the neck!"

In this manner, we use words that are present in our language and vocabulary. Now it is time to create your vocabulary on the basis of your inner experience. When you return to your inner experience (heart, *tejasthan* or bright place) and remain there, the words that emerge will make you wonder from where such words could emerge! "How did such a composition of words take shape? Never did such compositions emerge before!" In this way, instead of speaking on the basis of your beliefs, begin to speak on the basis of your inner experience.

When a poet composes an exquisite piece of poetry, he himself is amazed. He wonders, 'How did such a lovely piece of poetry emerge from me! How did such a beautiful composition of words take place?' The poet knows the words but not how to combine and compose them. As soon as he moves away from his ego and reaches the heart (*tejasthan*, bright place), such compositions begin to emerge and on hearing which he himself is wonderstruck. You too need to understand these secrets and imbibe them. On implementing these secrets in life, you will witness many wonders within yourself.

After knowing the five supreme secrets of life, set a goal according to your understanding, and remain steadfastly and unwaveringly committed to it.

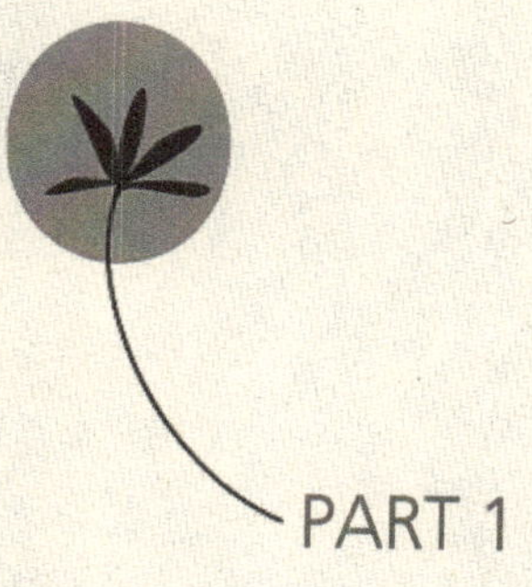

PART 1

First Supreme Secret of Life

Chapter One

The First Supreme Secret of Life

The Problem is not a Problem

On account of being a slave of the mind, man has been living with constant problems. Where do these problems come from? Why do they come? What is the solution to them? Do problems really come to trouble us? We do not have answers to these questions. How can we be liberated from problems? This question has become a riddle for us. One who knows the supreme secrets of life can easily solve this riddle, freeing himself from problems and creating a stress-free society.

Man feels he is beset with innumerable problems in life. But this is his misconception. There are not numerous problems, but only one. The first supreme secret of life states: '*To consider the events in our life to be a problem is the only problem.*'

Due to ignorance, man views events in life from a wrong perspective. His wrong perception makes him see only problems. What man needs to realise primarily is to stop considering a problem as a problem. As soon as he begins to view any incident as a 'problem', the situation deteriorates tenfold. Replacing the word 'problem' with 'challenge' helps to reduce the problem tenfold.

When man stops viewing incidents as problems, which is the

only problem, all problems cease to exist of their own accord. No incident can be considered a problem. On understanding this, all our problems disappear spontaneously. When we understand this first secret, all difficulties get eliminated and we stop looking at situations in life as problems. Along with this, we understand that we have to '*live our life in glory and not by being distraught due to problems.*' Being distraught is to demean ourself. Inside us is a glorious place which is called by different names — as heart, *tejasthan* (bright place), *maun* (silence), bright *knowlerience* (knowledge of self arising from inner experience). We should refrain from leading a tense life due to difficulties and thus disconnected from the glorious *tejasthan* and wonderful inner experience. We must learn to live with pride and not with ego. Pride is true while ego is false. For instance, people with false ego indulge in needless expenses like going for picnics, parties, taking loans, etc., such that their entire life is passed in paying for these.

Whenever we find an incident becoming a problem, in order to find relief from it, we can make use of the knowledge derived from the first secret and follow it up with the two steps given below:

First step: Give positive words to your feelings

Second step: Repeat the faith *mantra*

First step: Give positive words to your feelings. No incident is a problem but becomes one when you give negative words to your feelings, thus getting entangled in your own words. Whenever an incident occurs in life, you usually express your state verbally at the time of the incident. You express feelings in words by saying: "I am very scared... I am feeling insecure... I am shocked ... I am feeling bored... I am distressed... I am disappointed... I am very angry... I am extremely worried... I am feeling very disturbed... I am feeling anxious..." In this manner you give words to your feelings, but often these words are negative in nature.

When you repeat such negative sentences, you get stuck in your own words. Hence, when expressing your feelings verbally, remember to give positive words to them. By using wrong words to express your feelings, you begin to feel according to the way you say things. So instead of saying," I am feeling insecure", say, "I feel that it is necessary to be cautious here".

Instead of fear or insecurity, if you were to choose positive words to express your feelings, then the negative words would stop troubling you. However, do exercise some caution whenever you feel insecure. 'Got sacred' or 'felt insecure' — such phrases begin to generate negative feelings. So the next time you express your feelings, stop for a moment to ask yourself, 'What words should I use to express my feelings?' If you use the right words, you will not suffer from the resultant unhappiness. But in such a state, people use negative words for their feelings and start feeling miserable. They fail to realise that the cause of their unhappiness is their own words.

If, to express our feelings, we use the word 'problem', then the problem begins to manifest with this word itself. Instead of the word 'problem', if we were to say, "The incident that is taking place now has a solution, a gift, a ladder, a lesson and a challenge. This incident poses a challenge for me; it has come to teach me a lesson or to become a ladder for my progress. I feel it has come to give a solution and a gift," the incident will no longer appear a problem. If we use the right words to express our feelings, we learn to accept every situation as a challenge and express ourselves to the full and enjoy it. Hence, when confronting a problem, we must work on our feelings in the right manner and in true faith.

A negative feeling arises only to convey that what does not happen every time or every day is happening now. If we feel it, we give words to that feeling. A feeling arises just to convey that something good or something bad is occurring. By giving words to it, we do not have to get entangled in it. Whenever any feeling arises, we should replace that negative feeling with faith. The aim of the feeling is to convey the state we are in. The role of faith is to keep that state in control.

Our feeling tells us about our state while faith keeps it in control. It is like a person keeping a thermometer under his tongue to check his fever. Medicines keep the fever under control. In the same manner, a feeling conveys that something is different today. The bright faith that is inside us keeps this feeling in check. This faith is our medicine. That is why we have to shift from negative feelings to faith. The feeling will play its role in conveying our present state, which is different from what it was on other days. When an incident occurs which is different and which does not feel good, we usually tend to cling to this feeling and keep crying. This is because our reach is restricted to the bodily (physical plus mental) feelings. We are not aware of the internal feeling, which is beyond the body-mind. Hence we get stuck with the feelings of the body-mind. But now, without getting stuck in such feelings, we need to take a different step that will increase the power of faith in us.

Second step: In the second step we need to repeat the faith *mantra* with full concentration and belief. The faith *mantra* is: 'I can tackle this challenge; the power to tackle has been within me since the very beginning.'

When the faith *mantra* is repeated in times of difficulty, we instantly come out of the negative feeling associated with the difficulty. The faith within us is the strength that can control our negative feelings. Our feeling expresses the current state we are in.

Indication of the hand

Whenever we face a problem, we must question ourselves: 'What is this incident actually? What is hidden in this problem? What is the secret behind it?' The five fingers of our hand will provide the answer (*see* picture on p. 9).

Chapter Two

The Solution Lies in the Problem Itself

First Secret, First Finger — Solution

If seen in the right perspective, every incident proves instrumental in our progress. This is indicated through the five fingers of the hand. The little finger of the hand is the most subtle and the smallest. Hence it is used to indicate the 'solution', which, though present, is not easily discernible. This means that every problem has a solution, but we need to work on the solution to the problem. The solution lies hidden within the problem itself.

Once a person lost his horse. He inserted an advertisement in newspapers announcing that anyone who could find his horse would be awarded Rs 5,000. People went in search of the horse, but no one could find it. At last a young lad found the horse and brought it to the owner. When asked how he had found the horse, the boy replied, "I said to myself, 'if I were a horse, where would I go?' I went to that place and found the horse present at that spot."

To be able to think from another's viewpoint is a very subtle quality. Only when we step into another's shoes (the horse's shoe in this case) can we enter that feeling, that state, in which the other is.

When we penetrate the thinking of any person, only then can we learn of what the person feels. Thinking from another's perspective is an art.

People often complain that whenever they meet a new person, they are unable to find a topic of discussion. The obvious solution to this is: When we put ourself in the other person's shoes, we can see what that person will eat, drink, like, dislike, what his problems are, etc. This way we gain some information about him and face no difficulty in conversing with him. Based on the information acquired, we can ask him any number of questions. Stepping into another person's shoes, you think, 'Where will I go now?' Based on this thought, we can ask the person, "Where are you planning to go now?" The person will then give us some reply, based on which we can begin a conversation. As we continue to delve further, we will begin to extract more and more topics to discuss. Initially we might find it a bit difficult, but later, when we learn to find solutions, it will become easier.

The solution to a problem lies in the problem itself. This means that the cure to a disease is in the disease itself, just as the answer to a question is in the question itself. When our body is unable to digest a particular fruit, we need to remember that the solution lies in the fruit itself. Suppose, after eating a piece of watermelon, we begin to feel uneasy or unwell, then right then and there we can chew five or six watermelon seeds. Our problem will disappear. This means the problem emerged from the watermelon and so did the solution. If we do not eat the peel (skin) of a fruit, for example, if we eat the guava without its peel and our body is unable to digest it, then next time we must eat it along with its peel. If a fruit causes problems with the peel, then eat it after peeling. If a banana causes a problem, then after eating the banana, remove some pulp from the inner side of the peel and eat it. This will prevent any trouble caused due to the banana.

If stung by a scorpion, the antidote to the poison of the scorpion lies within the scorpion itself. The head of the scorpion can be cut and roasted in fire. The roasted ingredients can be applied to the wound and it would heal. In short, all that is needed is a person who has the right knowledge about preparing this medicine. Initially we may wonder about how the solution can lie within the problem or how could the answer to a question be found within the question itself! But this is a fact. In an examination, many students do not read the questions properly and end up giving the wrong answers. They then wonder why they receive a low percentage.

The same applies to our enemies. We can straightaway ask them how we can kill them. For example, in the epic *Mahabharata*, the warrior Bhishma was invincible. All plans to eliminate him failed. To win the war it was necessary to eliminate him. At that crucial juncture, Lord Krishna advised the Pandavas to go and ask Bhishma himself as to how he could be killed. To this Bhishma replied that he would never take up arms against a woman. It was then that a plan was hatched in which Arjun was shielded by Shikhandi (a eunuch) in his battle against Bhishma and Bhishma was defeated. Thus the idea emerged from Bhishma himself.

From this you can gather that to kill your enemy, or rather to eliminate the enmity, you can extract the solution from the enemy himself. Try to enter the shoes of your enemy and think. You will find the way to eliminate the enemy. Killing the enemy does not necessarily mean killing him bodily. Annihilating enmity is akin to killing the enemy. See things from the enemy's perspective — ask what he is feeling, why he is behaving so, what he has been through in life, etc. Only by thinking from the enemy's perspective can you eradicate enmity and hatred.

The little finger will remind you that the solution to every problem (however subtle it may be) is present within that problem. Therefore, whenever confronted with a problem, ask yourself which finger you should use — the first or the second.

You have many options. In spite of this, you complain, 'I am unable to find a solution to my problem.' On the contrary, make use of every option available to solve it and become creative. You have the solution to your problem on your fingers, but you are unaware of the solution. The little finger will remind you, 'The solution to a problem is in the problem itself.' And the first supreme secret will remind you: '*To consider a situation as a problem is the only problem.*'

Thus we have to learn to look at a problem correctly. In this manner, every problem in life, or every illness, can be eradicated. This can be further explained through a few more examples. When we put our hand in the fire, the hand gets burned. If someone were to say that he does not believe in this, then he can be explicitly told, "Fine. Don't believe it. But it is a fact." Nature does not depend on his believing in it or not. There are the laws of life — some known and some unknown, which are at work. Some people believe in them and some do not. We have neither to believe or disbelieve; we simply have to know them.

In another example, a person complained to his friend, "Your cow entered my fields and chewed up all my vegetables. It was a big loss for me."

The friend replied, "Fine. I will send you some milk from the cow that ate your vegetables. In this way the vegetables that the cow ate will be compensated for."

The problem was the cow and the solution also emerged from the cow.

Often many great scientists fail to find a simple solution to a problem, whereas an ordinary person unknowingly ends up making a great discovery. A person was travelling in a car. On the way, one of the tyres got punctured. He removed the four nuts of the tyre and kept them aside. But these fell off into a drain flowing along the edge of the road. Now he did not know what to do.

A young boy passing by asked him, "What is the matter? Can I help you?"

The person looked at the boy and did not feel that the boy could help him. Nevertheless, he narrated what had happened. The boy replied, "Nothing to worry about! Just take out one nut each from the remaining three tyres and use them to fasten this tyre. In this way your car will safely reach the mechanic's garage at least."

The person was taken aback. The solution was so simple. It did not require a highly developed intellect; all it needed was some commonsense. Thus, the problem came from the car and so did the solution. The nuts came from the car itself.

Now if you are confronted with any problem, do not get tense. Stop for a while and try to find a solution from within the problem. In the beginning it will be difficult to understand this and finding a solution may be very tricky. But as your faith increases, this fact begins to manifest itself. This rule plays a big role in our life.

Crime detectives know that in order to catch the criminal they must first check out the crime scene. The criminal's clues are sought at the place of the crime, because that is where the criminal is often found to return after committing the crime. Detectives know this law of life and are able to find a solution at the scene of the crime many a times.

In a kingdom, a burglary took place for the first time. No burglary had ever taken place before. The king asked the minister, "What kind of a problem is this? There has been a theft here; do something!"

The minister replied he would look into the matter. He went to the scene of the burglary and closely studied the scene before announcing his verdict, "Let the door of the house be punished by inflicting 50 whiplashes on it."

This news spread all over the kingdom and everybody wondered how whipping the door could solve the problem. The door was nevertheless whipped in front of all who had gathered. In the middle of the proceedings, the minister interjected, "Stop. I will now ask the door. Let me see if it gives me the right answer." The minister put his ear intently to the door for some time and then announced, "The door has revealed everything that took place and has told me who the thief is. The thief is the one who has cobwebs stuck to his head."

At that moment a person immediately raised his hand to check his head. He was caught on the spot. The stolen goods were found in his house.

In another instance, a teacher posed a question to his students, "There are two pots. One is filled with water and the other with alcohol. If a donkey comes near, what will it drink — the water or the alcohol?"

A boy raised his hand and answered, "It will drink water."

The teacher was pleased with the answer and asked him,

"How did you know that it will drink water and not alcohol?"

The boy replied, "You yourself said that it was a donkey. The donkey has no brains! Being a donkey, it will only drink water. You gave away the answer in the question itself, so what's there to think?" Thus the question itself can provide the answer.

Once, a huge python entered a village. It began to feed on the sheep belonging to the villagers by swallowing them whole. It did not even spare human beings. The people lived in fear and danger. A magician also lived in the village. The villagers approached him to seek his help in overpowering this dangerous creature. He said, "I cannot kill the python. But I know a technique, with the help of which I can find a person who can kill the python."

The villagers replied, "So be it. Tell us what you know."

The magician said, "I will tell you. But first let me find such a person."

After a few days he brought a person along with him and said, "He will kill the python."

And indeed, this man killed the python. All the villagers were overjoyed. When the magician was asked how he had found the right man to kill the python, the magician replied, "I know a law which states that the solution to a problem lies within the problem. I myself took the form of a python and sat by the bridge of the river. On seeing me, passers by ran away in fear. Only one man stood fearlessly. On seeing this, I returned to my original form of a human being and requested that man to help us solve the problem."

In this way, in order to fight the python, the magician solved the problem by becoming a python himself.

Initially, this secret may appear to be odd and difficult to understand. However, with repeated reading and contemplation, you will be able to gain useful insight and it will help you a lot while facing problems in your life.

Chapter Three

Seek the Shifting and not just the Solution

High and Right Perspective

To search for a solution to a problem is not the true solution. The true solution lies *in making space for the solution to emerge.* When we are disturbed over a problem, we get constricted. As a result, the solution to the problem gets obstructed, much to our disappointment. *When we realise that we don't have to look for the solution,* then we have found *the true solution.*

With every problem, man tries to find a solution to overcome it. A troubled mind is unable to find simple solutions to simple problems. When the mind calms down, the solution emerges. The solution to every problem invariably follows the problem just as day follows night. On falling ill, man takes treatment and rest. Similarly, in order to find a solution to the problem, it is essential to remain tension-free. No sooner does tension disappear, then the solution becomes clearly visible. More than searching for the solution, it is essential to go to our centre (our *tejasthan*, the heart). By getting confused in thoughts, we complicate the simplest of solutions. Understanding this fact can help us overcome our problems.

When a problem first crops up, shift your attention away from the problem and calm yourself. Shifting your attention is an art. People who can shift focus and whose perspective changes, say, "It is easy to shift the focus — to focus the mind on the heart. Where is it difficult to meditate? Why are people not able to understand this?" But people who are unable to do this, ask, "Why am I not able to see this?"

When someone sees an image take form in the clouds, he says, "I can see a chariot there," but you contradict and say, "I can't see it." From which angle is the person able to see an image in the clouds? Once you are able to identify the angle, the perspective, you will find that it is so easy.

Whenever an opportunity arises to render service or undertake a task, ask yourself what you learnt from your past experience. Then think, 'What intention should I have to learn this time? Before this task gets completed, I should get the answer to this question of mine or attain a solution to this particular problem so as to break my pattern. If I usually get upset at someone's unpleasant words, then at today's service I should get the opportunity to work on my patience with words. When people don't use the right words with me, I need to to be more patient with them.'

When you take up an intention and then work, what will happen? When someone does not speak properly to you, then by exercising patience you would feel happy, thinking, 'My intention is getting fulfilled. Someone is helping me, because this was my aim for today.'

However, if on that day everyone speaks sweetly to you, what would you think? You will think, 'Today everyone spoke nicely to me and so my day's intention was not fulfilled. I wanted to check what would happen to me when someone spoke improperly to me. I wanted to see how on such an occasion I could shift to *maun*, the inner experience.' That particular day everyone spoke well with you, but just as you were about to leave for the day, someone spoke rudely. For you that person becomes the most important person of the day. This is called shifting (high and right perspective).

'Shifting' means that what was once felt wrong now feels right.

If something which was a cause for sorrow once now becomes a cause for happiness, it is called shifting. Most people believe that problems arise due to other people and it is others who need to change. If you too subscribe to the same belief, then even if you were to work more than Edison, you will not succeed because your direction itself is wrong. If you work in the right direction, then no matter where you are, the door to the solution will open up right there. If your mind follows the right direction, the door appears right where you are.

Once you learn this secret, then every lane in the maze a door appears for you to emerge from. On learning about this secret, your reaction is: 'Should I come out now or should I take a few rounds? Since I have entered the maze, I might as well see what's in it? What surprises does it contain? What is the magic? How does man get entangled in it? Let me find how this maze was created.' This is called 'shifting'. Earlier you lamented this, saying, "It's a maze; it is very troublesome. It is causing a lot of difficulties and frightening me." But, as soon as the supreme secret is revealed, all problems disappear. Thus the solution to every problem lies with you. All you need to do is change your perspective.

There is a story about a thief who joined a traveller on his journey. At night, when he got an opportunity, he began to search the traveller's belongings with the intention of robbing him of his money. But he failed to find anything. Next morning he revealed his true identity to the traveller and said, "I know you are carrying money. At night, I searched your belongings, but could not find any money. Now that I am leaving, can you tell me where you have hidden it?"

The traveller revealed the secret, "I kept my money under your pillow. I knew that you would look everywhere except under your pillow."

From this you can conclude that the solution to any problem follows you all the time. You tend to look everywhere except where it exactly is. It is no wonder that what is generally told to a person, who is trying to medidate, is, "Turn around; where is your attention?" This gives him the opportunity to seek shifting, that his attention should not be directed anywhere else but within.

What we need is shifting and not just the solution. To look for a solution, we need not go too far. We just need to attain shifting. No matter what difficulties or miseries we face today, all we need to do is to bring about shifting in them. Avoid saying, "I want a solution." Instead, say, "I want shifting." If an incident seems painful to you, then that itself indicates that you need a new perspective. However, if you feel good in a similar situation, it means that you have already received a shifting.

What do you want? Do you want a solution or shifting? On what sort of problems do you need a shifting? Here you must ask yourself what causes distress to you. You will yourself discover the causes. You may be asked if a solution should be given to you to solve the problem or would you prefer to get a shifting? If you feel a particular person is a snob, then would you like his snobbery to be curbed or take recourse to shifting? If you say, "I feel that this person is useless," then should that person be made useful or would you prefer a shifting? Ideally, when you get a shifting, you can say from a new perspective, "He is a very useful person. In fact, he's just right for this work (of not doing anything). There is no need to remove him."

In life even those people who are not of any use have a role to play. This is a shifting. If you had not received this shifting, you would have said, "He is useless; so fire him." But you do not say this because the person has a role to play in your life; albeit of a slightly different nature, which is not apparent at once. The work or service rendered by some people is visible instantly. A well-defined task comes to the forefront immediately as seen in a person who organises an event or a person who teaches, etc. But the work of some others is not so apparent.

In some persons, a subtle expression of the self (Universal Self) goes on. Those who make arrangements will want to make arrangements of many kinds. But when you simply don't know about a particular thing, how would you arrange for it? You need to know that persons are also required who are of no use. Only then will you arrange for such persons or search for them and induct them in.

Labelling a person or a situation as being right or wrong leads to unhappiness. If you attach the right labels, such as, "This is required now, that will be required later," then the question of anything being wrong does not arise. "This path leads to that particular direction. The other path leads to the opposite direction." So there is no question of anything being wrong. Once you attain shifting, then in every incident, with every person, as soon as the mind begins to say something, you will say to it, "You need a shifting; not a solution." You tend to pray for this or that to happen when actually all you need is shifting. You should recognise this at once.

A patient may beg, "Give me sweets. Give me sweets..." But the doctor knows what the patient needs as the doctor has seen his blood report. The patient may insist but he will be told firmly, "No. You do not need sweets; you need to eat bitter gourd." (Bitter gourd juice is useful in treating diabetes.) The patient may not agree at first and plead, "Give me a banana, but not bitter gourd. It's fine if you keep me alone.But don't put me with that person. I will do this work alone but not with that person." But the blood report reveals the role of bitter gourd or the role of that useless person in your life. Since he is useless, you will find what kind of feelings arise in you on seeing him, which otherwise are present but remain hidden. Feelings of anger, hatred, jealousy, etc. may come to light. Only when such negative qualities come to light will you be made aware of what lies within you. Only then would you think of getting rid of these evils of the mind. At the same time the useless person will help you develop qualities like patience, self-control, self-discipline, understanding differences, teaching attitude, etc. You need such a person for this very purpose, otherwise you would never be able to learn about your negative aspects and develop the positive qualities mentioned above. If this useless person makes you aware about certain aspects hidden within you and also helps you develop your qualities, then how is he useless? If the useful is valued due to the existence of the useless, then how is the so-called 'useless' useless? Since beauty comes into prominence due to the existence of ugliness, then why should ugliness be banished from the world? Thus everything in the universe is useful; nothing is useless, not even the useless. This is shifting.

You should get this shifting done as soon as possible. Everybody needs it, although in different words. Ask yourself the question, "W or N?" every time you go shopping. 'N' stands for 'need' and 'W' stands for 'want'. There are many wants, but the need is only one. There is only the need for shifting. If the need is fulfilled, then wants seem like a bonus. Once your wants get fulfilled, then say, "I have got my bonus."

Chapter Four

Search for the Gift Hidden in Every Problem

The First Secret, Second Finger — Fruit

The second finger is associated with the fruit resulting from an incident. The second finger is the ring finger, where the ring is worn. This finger will remind you of the fruit of any incident. Every deed yields a fruit. Every problem arrives with a gift. A problem comes with the sole purpose of giving you a gift, but man, out of ignorance, keeps crying all his life over problems. If man knew how to handle problems, he would have been able to see the gift lying within the problem. By just thinking about or seeing many problems, man becomes unhappy. He becomes unhappy when a relative dies, or a friend falls ill, or he does not get a promotion, or he is sacked from his job, or his child fails in an examination, and so forth. If a person looks back and analyses the problems in his past, he would realise that each incident that seemed to be a problem had in fact given him a gift. He will realise how beautifully everything was going on and how futile was his anxiety. From this, one has to make attempts to search for a gift in every problem since every problem has not only a solution within but also a gift. Every problem that comes in life brings a gift along with it. People in whose life problems do not arrive remain dull and stupid throughout life. Only those who face problems move ahead in life.

Plants that face many a storm grow into strong trees, but plants that never have to deal with a storm grow up to become trees that get uprooted by the first storm they face. Plants that face and endure many a storm (problem) become strong enough to face the strongest of winds that may blow, as it would make no difference to them. Hence it has been said, "With every problem arrives a gift."

Whenever a problem crops up, keep two things in mind. First ask, 'What is the gift in it for me?' The gift is always present in the problem; all you need is to notice it. That eye, that perspective, is being given to you. The perspective of seeing the truth is being granted so that it becomes easy to dissolve problems. The second point to remember is that the solution to the problem lies within the problem. All you need to do is to awaken your awareness to be able to grasp it.

Once you carry out the exercise of dissolving the problem, you will find yourself receiving a very big gift. The more you see this gift, the more your happiness will grow. Till date you must have received many a gift on your birthday, wedding anniversary, festival, party, etc. On opening the gifts, how happy you must have felt. You may have remarked, "Wow! What a nice gift!" The next day you may have opened the gift to look again at it. Do you feel the same sense of happiness as you felt the first time? You will see that you do not feel the same degree of happiness. Open the gift again on the third day...the fourth day...Gradually you will observe that your happiness keeps on decreasing and after a few days you will even fail to acknowledge its presence. You may display it in a showcase or store it away in the attic. Now you do not even look at it. Each of you must have experienced this.

If you get to the root of the problem, you will discover a gift there — a gift on opening which, every time, your joy increases. Your happiness will keep growing day by day. You can receive such a gift. This gift lies behind your thoughts.

In the next chapter, let us look at the problems that arise from these thoughts and find the solution as also the gift present behind the thoughts.

As soon as you understand the problem, its solution becomes visible. Only after seeing the fire of the problem raging in a burning house will you be able to find the way out of the problem.

Chapter Five

Your Problem is a Stepping-stone

The First Secret, Third Finger — Ladder

The third finger (middle finger) indicates that there is a ladder in every problem. This can be compared to a springboard used to dive into the water. Depending on how deep the dive to be made is, the diving board is placed. The bigger the leap, the higher the springboard is placed. The springboard is thus made according to the diver who wants to dive in that pool. Just like the springboard, every problem is a ladder, which proves instrumental in helping you take a leap into success. If you are able to make your problem the right medium, you can climb the ladder of success and scale the peak of self-expression. The peak of self-expression (expression of the true self) is scaled only through problems. Hence, treat every problem as an opportunity.

Consider every problem an opportunity to express the godly qualities present within you and derive happiness from them. Soon you will realise that you tend to contemplate upon problems only due to incidents that do not occur in your daily life but happen only once in a while. In your daily routine life, you never sit down to contemplate.

Your entire life is spent just like the bull, which is tied to a peg and walks round and round it. The bull is used to extract oil from groundnut seeds and to prevent it from feeling giddy, its eyes are covered on the outer corners so that it cannot see on either side. It can only see in the front, thereby making it feel that it is going somewhere. Thus it keeps on walking round and round without getting anywhere. Similarly, our life goes round and round in circles in our daily routine. Problems arrive to awaken us. Treating each of them as a stepping-stone or a springboard, we must move ahead. In order to cross a marshy patch, we tend to drop a stone in it and use it as a stepping-stone to cross over the patch and move ahead. Similarly the problem too is a stepping-stone on which we can step and go across.

You have come to Earth to fulfil a purpose. Be careful lest you forget the purpose in worthless pursuits. When any problem bothers you, ask yourself why it is obstructing you before treating it as an instrument, a medium. Your journey should not stop because of the problem. It would indeed be a great loss if even after being given such a precious opportunity, of a human birth, you were to get stuck midway on the journey by not making use of the opportunity.

Once you understand the true significance of problems in your life, every problem that you confront will seem like a gift to you. You will begin to say, "It's good that it has happened so! If the problem (fights between husband and wife, problems regarding children, losing a job, job transfer, illness, etc.) had not cropped up, I could not have moved ahead. I was about to stop praying, thinking, contemplating, listening to the truth, walking the path of truth and helping others." Hence, whenever a problem arises, then without getting troubled, treat the problem as your ladder. You need to realise that the problem is essential to keep you awake. Otherwise man would fall asleep, living unconsciously and believing himself to be very knowledgeable. Instead of dissolving his problems, he would drown in them.

Life in this world brings all kinds of problems in its wake. Unmarried persons have different problems; married people have different ones; those who have children have different problems; those who do not have children have other problems. Everybody has different problems and different questions. The problems of some are related to children, job or business, whereas the problems of some others are related to mental issues such as fear, stress, worry, anger, etc. What we need to understand is that problems have to be treated as an instrument of our growth. When we stop on the path of progress, then life introduces some problems to awaken us, else man does not want to move ahead. For complete development, we should not treat problems as troublesome but use them as stepping-stones or springboards. By stepping on problems, we can take a leap to reach the peak of progress.

Stress becomes our strength and anger becomes our energy once we learn to understand the supreme secrets of life. A certain amount of stress is essential to carry out a specified task within a specified time. Otherwise due to lethargy, the body and mind try to avoid work as far as possible. This is particularly true for those people who are lethargic by nature. An optimum level of stress creates a state wherein the body-mind begin to work fast and with complete focus. This is particularly apparent during work deadlines or examinations. Thus this stress can become one's source of strength. Just avoid getting over-stressed. Do not look at stress as a problem, but as a ladder, which helps you do your best in a given situation and emerge with flying colours. Thus, whenever you feel any stress, rest assured that it has arisen to extract something out of you. Just watch what is that. Once you adopt this attitude towards stress, you would never feels stressed.

Similarly, anger is not merely destructive but is Nature's way of endowing us with energy. It depends on us how we use this energy. Fire is energy, which can be used for cooking food or for burning others' homes. It is the same with anger, which can be used either destructively or constructively. If we learn to make constructive use of this energy, we can be successful in extracting constructive results from anger, but we need to learn this art. If anger arises and we start investigating, then it becomes investigative anger. A distressed person gets very angry and tries all kinds of ways and means to end his distress. Many scientific discoveries have been the result of investigative anger. Whenever the rulers of a nation or kingdom exploited their subjects, the subjects revolted in anger, leading to a revolution. If there had been no anger (violent or non-violent) in freedom fighters of colonised countries, perhaps they could not have obtained freedom from their rulers. This means that when anger is used as per the needs of the situation with full awareness, it becomes a great power. With anger, the doors of truth can be opened. A seeker's anger is most powerful. It arises out of the questions: 'How much longer can I live in ignorance? Till when shall I burn in the fire of hatred and misery?' Because of such questions, his search begins. This is the use of anger. Even self-realisation becomes possible. Thus, problems such as stress and anger can also become ladders for our progress.

Chapter Six

Every Problem Presents a Beautiful Lesson

The First Secret, Index Finger — Lesson

To be liberated from problems, the index finger indicates a lesson. A problem is not a trouble-maker, but a tutor. In every problem there lies a hidden lesson.

For explaining a point, the index finger is used. When a teacher or a master wishes to teach something, he uses the index finger to convey his point. This finger is associated with 'lesson'. You too can acquire your lesson from every problem by remembering this finger. What do you learn from a problem? Do you learn any lesson?

If we learn from every problem, if every problem comes with a lesson, then the index finger reminds us to learn the lesson. Suppose a person confronting a financial problem learns to save money, then the habit of saving can forever free him from monetary problems. In case a person faces a financial problem, but having understood the first secret, asks himself, 'What lesson is ingrained for me in this problem?' he then learns proper planning and use of his finances and investment. He also develops respect for money — the habit of saving and not spending on worthless pursuits. Have *you* learnt this lesson?

When somebody faces a health problem and becomes a victim of some illness, he can learn from his illness too. He may learn the importance of regular physical exercise so as to maintain good health for the rest of his life. Have *you* learnt the importance of regular exercise?

A person is unable to complete his work on time. All his tasks remain incomplete. From this problem, he learns how to manage and plan his time (time management). This way his work will get completed well before time and he can enjoy success in life. Have *you* learnt the art of time management?

There can be a person who is a victim of misunderstandings in his relationships. Friends and acquaintances are unable to understand him. Due to this problem, if he learns the art of expressing himself clearly and also the importance of communication, then this lesson provides him with the benefit of enjoying pleasant relationships. Beneath this issue lies the lesson of human psychology and human relations which teach him to live in harmony with others. Have *you* understood the cause of misunderstandings in your relationships? Have *you* learnt the art of strengthening relationships? If not, then this problem will keep recurring in your life.

A person may never be able to locate his keys on time. He wastes time in searching for things. Due to this problem, he realises the importance of keeping things in their place. There should be a system and a place to keep things at home, in office and in business. Due to his problem of misplacing things, he learns the lesson to keep everything in its proper place. This goes to show that he truly learns to utilise the first secret. Have *you* imbibed this lesson in your life? If so, then you will save a lot of time in your life. But there are many persons who waste a lot of time over searching for things.

A person may get agitated by the fact that he is unable to recall the idea which had occurred to him a day earlier and because of which he incurs a huge loss. He is unable to make progress in his business as he fails to recall that particular idea. If, from this problem he learns to develop the habit of writing things down, then he will learn to give shape to his creative ideas throughout his life. Do *you* write down every idea, every positive thought and *your* ultimate aim in life? If not, then *you* will not be able to achieve any major success in life.

A student may get tense during an examination as he has not studied his lessons. From this he should draw the lesson of developing the habit of preparing well before the exams. Once he learns the lesson of not postponing things to tomorrow, he is able to undertake his impending examinations without stress. Have *you* developed the habit of completing things while there is still time? If not, then *you* cannot expect to get freedom from stress.

If a person has the problem of often going into depression, then he should learn the lesson that he might improve by learning meditation. How can one meditate? How can one recognise one's true self? How does he surrender himself to Divine devotion? How does one surrender his stress, problems and worries to the higher power? Once he learns the art of meditation, he learns to live his entire life in the bliss of divine devotion. Have *you* learnt this lesson? If not, then *you* cannot attain everlasting happiness in life.

All the above-mentioned lessons have to be learnt. Have *you* learnt them? If not, then become alert before any problem confronts you. Develop those qualities in your body-mind due to which your time and money can be saved and you can accomplish what you want. You will be able to communicate properly with people while people will understand you as you will understand them. Learn good habits from every problem and attain health, wealth, success, love and happiness.

Have you learnt a lesson from your problem?
If not, become alert before any problem arrives
and develop good qualities in your body-mind.

Chapter Seven

Treat Every Problem as a Challenge

First Secret, Thumb — A Big Challenge

When we play a game, we do not say, 'Why should I stand in this very position? Why should I stay between these two lines? Why can't I run anywhere else? Why is there such a limitation in this game?' This is because we have been given these boundary lines within which we are expected to play so as to make the game interesting and exciting.

Here questions might arise: 'Why are we attached to a single body? Why can't we go outside it?' The answer is that this boundary of the body (the limitation) is a rule of the game being played on Earth, which poses a challenge to you. The purpose of this challenge is to derive maximum joy from the game. In spite of this challenge, if you want to know the secrets underlying the universe and if you are able to learn them, it is said that you have become an expert in the game. In spite of the limitations, such as lack of finance, pain in the body, people's taunts, lack of strength, shortage of time, time spent on earning your bread and so on, if you are able to express your true self, you will be called a successful player. In order to become a successful player in the game of life, learn to accept the challenge of your limitations.

In a game of carrom, you accept the rule of playing by staying between two lines. By using the striker placed between the two limiting lines, you need to pocket the carrom discs or coins. Similarly you need to accept this challenge of being within the body and becoming an expert at this game of life.

Initially you will find it troublesome and may feel, 'I cannot do this; it's not possible.' But gradually, as you keep trying through regular practice, you will see that every challenge becomes a rung on the ladder of success.

In this world, there are many who are deaf, dumb, blind or handicapped in some way and encounter difficulties. Such people should learn to treat the difficulties as a challenge. Those who do not face such problems, should treat it as a great responsibility on them. If they are free of problems, they should help those who are facing problems. Those who find liberation from problems learn to accept more problems. This means they invite the problems of others towards themselves. Is this not interesting? Those who do not have problems should learn to accept that their responsibilities have now increased. They now become a medium for others to help them emerge from their problems. Express gratitude to God for being free of all problems and accept those of others as a new challenge.

Once you learn to view every problem as an opportunity and realise your responsibility, accept the challenge, become instrumental in helping others, learn your lesson, climb the ladder, reach the pinnacle of progress, find the solution to the problem and receive a gift from it, then any problem will appear like no problem at all. Then the only problem of man, i.e. considering an incident as a problem, will vanish.

To become a successful player in the game of life, learn to accept your limitations, your challenges.

Chapter Eight

How to Attain Peace During Problems

Do Nothing and Neither Do the Task of Doing Nothing

When fights take place between members of the family, sometimes man is unable to exercise control over his thoughts. What should he do to overcome such unhappy thoughts? What should he do to solve his problem?

To be able to solve problems, man should be in the right mental state. If there is a storm of thoughts brewing in his mind, then the mind will not be able to see the solution, the gift, the ladder, the lesson, the challenge, the medium or the present. The dust from the storm blurs the mirror of the mind. At such a moment, the mind needs to be given time to pacify the storm inside. One should do nothing. Nor get entangled in finding how to do nothing! Try to understand this through an example. When a ship is caught in a storm and is unable to steer ahead, the captain of the ship releases the anchor of the ship into the water. The anchor is used till the storm does not ebb. This is the period of doing nothing. If at this time the journey is continued, there is danger of the ship sinking. On the arrival of a storm of problems, if your faith begins to sink, take the decision of 'doing nothing'. During this period of doing nothing, just observe your thoughts. Notice the waves of thoughts as an impartial observer or witness. By looking at your thoughts in this manner, the power of negative thoughts weakens and lost faith is regained. Being a witness means seeing from the *tejasthan* and doing nothing. On observing your thoughts from this place (*tejasthan*, bright place), the encouragement being given to thoughts also stops. Normally the mind does not let go of thoughts as it gets stuck to them.

Many meditation techniques have been devised to detach the mind from one's thoughts. In order to shift the focus from a problem, every technique is useful. At such times if you perform even a small meditation technique, it is of help as it takes the mind away from the problem. You can practice any technique you may have learnt. Close your eyes and focus on your breath, going in and out, or observe your thoughts as if looking at passing clouds. You can also perform self-enquiry by asking yourself, 'This problem has appeared to whom? Exactly who is not able to shift his focus from the problem? In which part of the body the pain, tension or stress is located? Where is the pulsation felt? Where is the vibration felt that is causing distress?' At such a time, first make your body taut and then leave it loose. You can also lie down in *shavasana* ('corpse pose' — a yogic relaxation posture where a person lies down on his back and leaves his body loose like a dead body). You can drink some cold water, exercise rigorously, do some creative work with your instinctive mind, play with children, etc. as it will shift your focus away from the problem.

Meditation means doing nothing and also not attending to the task of doing nothing. It is the ultimate medicine to calm the storm of thoughts. If you have the habit of practicing meditation, once a problem arises, the mind learns to automatically go into a state of meditation. Due to this habit, many mistakes that would have occurred are avoided. Hence, do not imagine that 'doing nothing' (meditation) is not doing anything. This 'doing nothing' is equal to a lot.

Various meditation techniques can be learnt from books

on meditation. This way you learn how to focus on the breath, or how to catch different types of sounds in the surroundings, even the subtle ones, and many other important things. If you shift your focus from the incident to anywhere else, you will find that you have come out of the tension caused by the problem for some time. But this is only for some time. Later you need to find a permanent solution by attaining understanding regarding the following aspects: 'Why does this stress arise during problems? Why does the whistle of the pressure cooker blow? What does the whistle indicate? How can we be liberated from stress?'

Solving a problem by chanting a *mantra*

Whenever a problem appears, you can chant a *mantra*, not necessarily aloud, but softly with the movement of your tongue. In this *mantra*, you can chant some holy words, the name of God, the name of the truth that you have received from your spiritual master, or some holy words from a sacred text. You should cultivate the habit of chanting a *mantra* well in advance of facing any problem. You should cultivate the habit of exercising. Your aim should be to fulfil the purpose of life before death arrives. You should take advantage of the opportunity that comes your way before letting it slip by. Do some great work before the arrival of old age. This will keep you firm and unflinching in the face of any problem. Regular chanting of the *mantra* begins to positively affect the subconscious mind. So apart from benefiting by becoming liberated from the tension of the problem, you also benefit from the *mantra*.

Chant the name of God to awaken the power of Divine devotion

Whenever a problem arises, chant the name of God or your guru or visualise their face in your mind. You will find the tension associated with the problem vanish and the power of faith awaken. With the awakening of faith, the most difficult of tasks of the world get accomplished and the most difficult of issues get resolved. As soon as the face of God or your guru appears in front of you, the feeling of devotion awakens in you and you forget the tension regarding the problem. With the power of devotion, all the seen and unseen powers of the universe begin to work for you.

With the coming of the storm of problems, if your faith begins to sink, then the decision to do nothing is the best decision to take.

Chapter Nine

The Secret of Liberation from Problems

Attain Emotional Maturity

When you get agitated over something, ask yourself the question, 'For how long should I be distressed over something that is distressing me?' Depending upon the answer, be troubled for only that period of time and not any further. A thing should be given only that much value as much as it is worth. Try to understand this through the following example.

You go to the market to buy a matchbox and the shopkeeper tells you that the matchbox is worth five rupees. You tell the shopkeeper, "Five rupees is too much." If someone tries to sell you something that is worth less than a rupee for five rupees, then you will not buy that thing. You will not buy it because you know its actual worth. In the same manner, when a person calls you a fool and walks off or someone fails to perform the work you tell him to do, then ask yourself, 'For how long should I remain upset over this?' For example, a person calls you a hippo. You do not feel bad about it but later when you visit the zoo and see what a hippopotamus looks like, you tend to get very angry. You then begin to think, 'Let me see him tomorrow, then I'll call him a dinosaur, I'll call him this… I'll call him that…' You begin to think a lot many things and get unduly upset. If at this point of time you realise that you need to attain emotional maturity and give only that much value as its worth, then you will ask yourself, 'I am getting troubled over this. For how long can I remain troubled by this? How much value should I give to this matter?' You will receive the answer from within you, according to your understanding. Suppose you get the answer, 'I should be upset over this for at least ten minutes', then you will do so. It is okay to feel upset for ten minutes, but no more. Do not give it even one second extra more than the ten minutes. Give a thing only that much value as much as it is worth; no more.

The day you understand how much value you should give to what, you will become mature. People grow up physically but remain children from within. Having grown up physically, if there is no maturity inside, then we have not truly grown. You do not know how much you should be perturbed by a particular issue. 'Maturity' means knowing how we should behave over a particular incident. Have you developed this emotional maturity? If we understand when and where what has to be said and not said, where little has to be said and where more needs to be said, our understanding comes to be described as emotional maturity. After attaining emotional maturity, we decide on what value to give to what and how much time to spend in agony over a given matter. We should not waste more time than necessary over trivial issues. In order to attain the supreme aim of life, it is essential to develop emotional maturity.

For instance, you approach your neighbour to borrow some tomatoes. But the neighbour refuses, making some excuse. For how long should you remain anguished over this? You start ruminating, 'When she fell short of sugar, she borrowed two bowls of sugar from me. But now, when I ask for tomatoes, she says she doesn't have any.' You keep mulling over it and feel more and more offended. But now you need to ask yourself, 'I did not get any tomatoes from my neighbour. So how long should I be upset over this issue? Say, at least fifteen minutes.' That is fine. You can very well be upset over it for fifteen minutes, but not more.

When you do this, you find that when you receive the answer as fifteen minutes, you begin to feel that even fifteen minutes is too much of a value to devote to that particular issue. When we refuse to pay Rs 5 for the matchbox, the shopkeeper tells us, "Okay, take it for four rupees." But we begin to think, 'Is not four rupees also too much?' Till we learn the true worth, we keep on reducing the price. In this way we will learn to evaluate. This evaluation should be done before getting upset over a given issue. We need to decide on the value to give to a particular item.

We do a lot of evaluation in the market. When speaking, how many ideas we use! How much we exercise our brains! Likewise, learn to evaluate yourself. Then you will feel that being distressed for even fifteen minutes is too much. Subsequently you will reduce the time of being distressed over a problem. When we do this consciously, we find that we do not feel as unhappy as we did initially, because we learn that it is foolish to waste time over such a trivial matter. We realise the true worth of the matter and stop getting troubled over it. This will happen automatically after attaining emotional maturity.

May you develop the emotional maturity as soon as possible. You will then realise the true cause for landing in depression or in other feelings and emotions as it is due to unconsciousness. You will learn not to fall below your true dignity. Even when unconsciousness breaks, ignorance persists as you do not have the understanding and you will continue to get disturbed. Simply breaking away from unconsciousness is not enough; you need the right understanding of life and its supreme secrets.

The king rides the elephant that does not get disturbed

When an elephant passes through a street, dogs bark at it. But the elephant, unperturbed, walks on, knowing that it's just the barking of dogs. When such a massive animal passes through a street, how can dogs tolerate it quietly? They will certainly bark. The elephant knows this and so it is not bothered at all. Elephants that get disturbed and agitated over this are not chosen to undertake great tasks.

In the ancient era, people used to ride elephants to fight in the battlefield. Soldiers, commanders, the general and the king used the elephant to participate in the war. Do you know which elephant used to be chosen for the king? An elephant which would not be affected by noise, pain and inconvenience. In a battlefield, some arrows are likely to pierce and hurt, but the elephant should be such that it does not get disturbed by it. Similarly if you get disturbed when someone speaks ill of you, then you cannot be selected for the highest form of self-expression. Only those who know how to remain worry-free, unshakeable and calm are chosen for great deeds.

You may ask, 'Through which body does the self express its qualities?' The self (God) wants to experience itself through the body of human beings. I, the self, can experience and express itself only through such human bodies which remain steady in any situation. This means that the body God wants to ride on should first undergo training. For elephants that get disturbed, the *mahout* is told to first train them before the king can ride them.

In the same manner, do you want the truth to awaken in you or the God to awaken in you or God to ride your body? This implies that if you want God to express himself through your body, how you should prepare your body! Someone speaks ill of you and you get upset; someone praises you and you begin to dance. This means you are not a balanced person in different situations. In such a body, the self will not be able to stabilise. The day you realise this truth, you will learn to be calm and derive happiness in every situation.

One day a person approached Lord Buddha and started hurling abuses at him. But Buddha remained calm and undisturbed. The person continued to hurl abuses, without any effect whatsoever on Buddha. At last, that person got tired and left. Those standing around, asked Lord Buddha, "Why didn't you say anything to that person?"

The Buddha replied, "Hurling abuses is his style. Not accepting those abuses is my style. Everyone has his/her own style."

Each body in whom the truth (the self, God) manifests, finds expression in different ways. The Buddha asked, "If someone brings you gifts and you do not accept them, then what happens to those gifts? That person will take the gifts back with him, which means that the gifts will remain with that person. Similarly, the person who hurls abuses at me, has to take them back with him when I refuse to accept them. Hence the abuses remain with him."

There was another saint who had his own method, his own style. The same kind of incident occurred with him too as had occurred with the Buddha. However, he gave an answer to every abuse. When a person abused the saint, saying, "You are muck, a pig, a disgrace...," the saint kept taking the name of an eatable in return for every abuse. He answered, "Candy, chocolate, custard... " You may say that the saint should have kept quiet, because that is what is expected of a saint. But you have to understand that every action does not evoke the same kind of response from everyone. Everything can elicit a fresh, a new response. Every time, according to the circumstances and according to the person in front, the response of the enlightened varies.

The person who hurls abuses at some point of time is liable to get agitated on not receiving any response. If someone abuses you and you counter him by giving funny names to each abuse, then he is liable to get disturbed.

Feeling upset, while the abuser walked off in a huff, people asked the saint, "Why were you behaving so? Why were you saying 'candy', 'chocolate', etc. in answer to each of his abuses?"

The saint explained, "It is the rule of life: *'What we give, we will have to take the same some day.'* For every action of ours we have to reap the fruit some day. Whatever a man spits out, he has to swallow the same some day. So I thought that I should spit out what I want to swallow." The inference to draw from this story is that whatever you spit would get back to you. Hence, why not spit (do deeds) that you would want to swallow (to attain).

What do you want in life? Do you want to get distressed? No. So why give something which will create trouble in your life? Speak only those words that you want to hear from others. When we understand the secrets of life, then different responses will be produced in different situations.

On feeling troubled, go to the royal room, the Silence (*maun*) Room. In a state of complete inner silence, you will realise your true identity and your emotional maturity will increase. How much value should you give to an incident that is troubling you; what is its true worth? When you realise this, you will stop being troubled by it. This is the secret of liberation from troubles.

The king rides only that elephant which is worry-free, unshakeable and calm.

Chapter Ten

Prayer During Problems

The Importance of Prayer

When questions about different problems are asked, the only answer to all the problems you experience, is, "Pray." If you have already started praying, then the answer is, "Let the prayer continue." The power of prayer invariably works in your life. Pray consciously according to your understanding as of today. You must have prayed earlier too. You pray today too. But understand that a true prayer is that which you should do for the truth, because truth has power. With the help of that power, you not only need to come out of all your problems, but also get stabilised in true happiness. If this were to happen, then you will not lack anything in life. Hence, continue to pray for attaining the truth and getting liberated from problems. Do not forget to pray each night before sleeping. Continue the prayer after waking up in the morning, because early morning is the right time for that prayer to seep into the subconscious mind. Otherwise, in spare time, the outer mind (conscious mind or the doubting mind) does pray, but it also says, 'It doesn't look like this prayer will ever be fulfilled.'

Just before you get down to sleeping, your outer mind is a little tired and hence, a little calm. Just when you wake up, all the hustle and bustle of the day has yet to begin and hence the mind is a bit calm. Therefore, in both cases, the time is ideal for prayer. But this does not mean that you cannot pray if that time has passed. You can pray at any time. If you continue to listen to and read the truth, then over time every word will become a prayer.

There is power in prayer and that is the reason for reaching where you are today. Whether you were aware or not that you were offering the prayers, you reached this present state because of your prayers and hence this book is in your hands. You have the power of prayer in your hands. In fact, this power has been given to each and everyone of us since the very beginning. Along with the problem, the strength to bear it and its solution have been already given to you.

Even before the problem arises, its answer, its solution, is provided to you. You only need to go within and look for the answer. You will find it. If you have such a power, then you need to learn to use it. It should not happen that you possess the Aladdin's lamp and fail to use it. Prayer too is such a power that can be used not only for physical and mental problems, but also for spiritual problems where one can pray in order to stabilise one's self.

Pray to God (form or formless), a guru or any deity you have faith in. The results of prayer come from the power of faith. Then it does not matter whether you pray to a mountain, a sacred spring, a temple, a mosque, a church, at home, in a bus or anywhere else. It is only your faith in the higher power that matters. You should pray wherever your faith begins to manifest. Do not let it remain confined within you because the prayer of faith will begin to work then.

Keep faith in the power of truth and prayer because prayer does work. It dissolves problems. However, the mind wants to see instant results. When we pray, the mind immediately wants to check if anything is happening or not. The effect of prayer begins as soon as the prayer is done. However, we are able to see it only later.

The importance of positive thinking

Whatever you prayed for will start moving towards you and the prayer begins to work on you to prepare you to receive it. But ignorance of this whole process makes you indulge in reverse prayer or stop praying.

Then the thing you prayed for stops where it is. When troubled, you again begin to pray and again the result starts moving towards you. When the reverse prayer begins unconsciously, the result again stops in its tracks. Too much time is lost in this game.

So pray with faith, certain that the solution to the problem begins to move towards you. Avoid putting obstacles in its path by negative thinking. Let the solution, gift, ladder, lesson come through positive thinking and happy thoughts. The result stops moving towards you due to your mistuning. There is a tuning for everything. The answer to your prayer is coming towards you. It is just due to lack of understanding that negative thoughts and thoughts of ignorance keep churning inside man. Otherwise, Nature is working beautifully. In Nature, everything is positive; nothing is negative. Only in man there is the contrast mind which is the comparing, weighing and judging mind that splits everything into two — good or bad. This mind cannot wait patiently after the prayer has been made. In the interim, it begins to think negative thoughts, like 'I don't think I will get what I want. I don't think this prayer will work.' The mind begins to assume and the assumptions and doubts stop the solution and gift from coming to you. Due to your prayer, some things move towards you. It is the checking and judging mind that kills the happiness by continuously checking and rechecking, 'Let me check if happiness has come to me; let me make sure that happiness has truly come!' The actual problem is the 'mind'.

Prayer has immense power to put out the flames of worry and soften even a stone. It can calm a storm and bring a sinking ship ashore. Through prayer, not only are one's desires fulfilled, but one receives salvation too. Surrender your problems to God and rest assured that God will solve your problems in a suitable manner.

Prayer has so much power that a single prayer is enough to set one on the path of truth. Everything in the world can be changed. In times of crises, even doctors advise their patients to pray when they find that they can do no more. Many a time we have heard a doctor remark, "This person was not going to survive. But God knows how he did!" The fact is that even today miracles can be witnessed when all seems dark and gloomy. The reason for this is that someone's prayer was continuously working to allow a positive situation to develop.

Whenever a calamity strikes or a problem troubles you, remember that before the problem, the solution to it has already been given to you. For example, even before a child is born, Nature arranges to provide milk for it. All that is needed is to look for the solution that lies within you. Prayer helps the solution to surface. By not making use of a supreme power, like the prayer, and by remaining lost in our ego, we commit a huge blunder. Hence the advice is to first pray whenever a problem crops up. Prayer is a supreme power that has been given to you. Make full use of it. When you cannot think of any solution in a difficult situation, turn to prayer. The solution would already be with you.

Whenever a calamity strikes or a problem troubles you, remember that before the problem, the solution to it has already been given to you.

Chapter Eleven

Laugh at Your Problems

The Soothing Ointment for Every Illness

It is easy to laugh when one is in a favourable state of mind with no problems troubling him. Even a fool can laugh in a favourable and enjoyable atmosphere. That's no big deal. However, laughing in times of adversity requires courage. If all our thirty-two teeth are in place and sparkling white, it is easy to laugh and is no big deal. But, if some of the front teeth are missing and yet you can laugh aloud with your mouth wide open, it requires courage. Laughing acts as a medicine in the cure for any illness. Hence it is often repeated that laughter is the best medicine. There are very few who can laugh at their problems and mistakes.

Two friends were studying together. While one was busy writing something, the other felt thirsty and picked up the jug of water kept in a corner of the study table. While pouring water into a glass, he inadvertently spilled some water on to the other's book. The book got entirely soaked in water. At this the first friend remarked, "It's fortunate that you don't drink ink."

The second friend was taken aback at this reaction and asked his friend what he meant. His friend explained, "This is only water. It will dry in some time. If you were drinking ink and spilled it, then my whole book would have been permanently spoiled." Both the friends began to laugh. You have just seen how by laughing, the atmosphere became light. No tension formed between the two and the problem too did not feel like a problem. Otherwise, in such a situation, a fight could have easily taken place between the two friends.

So come, let us resolve from today itself: '*Whenever we sense a problem, we will laugh at it*.' Only the wise know how to laugh at their own problems and follies. Laughing over your problems works like a soothing ointment. Whenever a problem emerges and you see yourself troubled by it, do laugh. If you cannot laugh, then, at least, try to smile. If Ajay faces a problem, then what will he do? Ajay will first smile and then say to himself, 'Ajay is unhappy. So let us see what Ajay does now.' Saying so, his smile will change to laughter. With laughter, the magnitude of the problem reduces and the solution becomes easily visible.

Laugh and the world will laugh with you. In order to solve problems, the support of the world is essential. With others' support even the toughest of tasks can be completed easily and in less time. By working with a smile, the problem gets solved faster and in the best possible manner.

Laughing at others is as easy as it is difficult to laugh at yourself.

Chapter Twelve

Your Problem is Instrumental for the World

Impersonal Problem

Whatever has been said in this book, do contemplate over it. When you face a problem, ask yourself, 'Has this problem appeared to anyone in the world before? Or am I the first one to face such a problem?' Reflect on this question.

When you ponder over your problem, do remember that many people prior to you have faced a similar problem. Also remember that because of this problem, later on some research or discovery is going to take place through your body. Even the discovery of truth took place in an effort to be liberated from problems.

Some people were constrained to live with blind persons who were their relatives. Going through the problems the blind faced, they later on did some good work for the benefit of the blind. They built shelters/homes for them. They were able to do this because they could empathise with the blind.

Due to the problems faced in life, we can very well feel what other people who are facing the same kind of problems must be going through. We get the thoughts to solve only those difficulties which we can empathise with. In this world, everyone has been given different kinds of problems to overcome, because each of them has a role to play in future in relation to these problems. Once we become aware of our role, then we stop getting tense over our problems. A girl named Helen Keller, who was deaf, dumb and blind, has set an exceptional example for us to follow. How can a deaf, dumb and blind person gain education? In spite of all her limitations, that girl not only got educated herself but even wrote books as she advanced in years. Even today, in every school for the blind, her name is the first to be mentioned. The blind students are told, "If Helen Keller can become an inspiration for the world in spite of being deaf, dumb and blind, then you too can do it, because you are only blind; not deaf and dumb too, like her." Today, the name of Helen Keller is an inspiration for the blind. How did this happen? Being deaf, dumb and blind was a big problem for Helen Keller at that time. But now we understand that by going through those problems, she was able to solve the problems of others.

If we look at our problem with understanding, we will be surprised to note that our problem is not ours at all. We have been given the problem so that others' problems are solved through it. Due to ignorance, we tend to treat a problem as our *own* problem. We develop attachment to our problem. We do not wish to come out of our unhappiness and may not even know how to do so.

When we look at our problem from this new perspective, we learn to treat our problem like a challenge. Solving the problem becomes our service to others. By solving our problem, we do a service to the world. When a person suffered from an incurable disease, he when about discovering a cure for it. He did succeed in finding the cure and became healthy. The discovery of that cure went on to cure millions of people affected by the same disease. Hence our problem is not ours at all. Our problem is not a problem but an impersonal challenge.

Until the work gets done through our body for which we have come to Earth, we will never experience fulfilment. Hence, we need to rethink the opportunity we have received. Rethink on the problem that you face. Think from a new perspective. Our problem is an impersonal problem. We need to realise this truth as early as possible. Hence, do not invite trouble by considering your problem to be a personal one. Imbibe the first supreme secret of life.

The higher the aim we set for ourselves, the greater is the strength that Nature provides us to achieve that aim. Hence, those who know the laws of Nature, never aim small.

Chapter Thirteen

How to Dissolve Problems all at Once

Understand Your truth, Dissolve Your Problems

In the initial chapters of the book we learnt about the first supreme secret of life. Now learn the art of dissolving your problems in no time.

On realising the truth, problems do not get solved, but are dissolved immediately. Till the time we do not know our true nature, we feel that all the problems we face are 'my' problems. But as soon as we know our true self, we realise that 'all these problems were not mine at all. They simply had no relation to me.' This is what is called the 'dissolving of problems all at once'. Understand this through the following:

A person parks his car by the side of the road and visits various stores. While hopping from one shop to another, suddenly he notices some people on the roadside, busy removing the wheels of his car and some others taking out things from the trunk. He is furious. He approaches them and tries to stop them, but they wave a knife at him and chase him away. In a state of great anguish and agitation, he rushes to a telephone booth to inform his friends and the police.

While speaking on the phone, his eyes fall on the number plate of the car. It suddenly strikes him that the car about which he was getting so disturbed, was not his car at all. His car was parked on the other side of the road. The two cars were similar in colour and shape. On realising his mistake, his problems vanish into thin air.

Man can be a victim of such a misunderstanding. He believes himself to be the body. When his body feels pain, he gets distressed at the thought that 'I' am in pain. When he realises all the secrets of life, he finds liberation from all his problems. Man uses his body. He is not this thing that he uses. Use the body, but do not get attached to it. It is similar to the person who believes some other car to be his own and gets worked up over it. On realising the truth, all his tension disappears. In the same manner, we can dissolve our problems immediately. Look at another example which gives a deeper understanding of the reality.

A person receives many bills one morning. He studies them all, one by one. The electricity bill... the telephone bill... the grocery bill... the laundry bill... a notice to pay the school fees of his child... and so on. Seeing the electricity bill, he calls a member of his family and screams at him, saying, "How much electricity you use! You switch on the geyser and forget to put it off. All day long you lie around, watching television. Just take a look at this electricity bill!"

Then he studies the next bill and calls the next member to rebuke, "How much milk do you consume? How much tea do you drink?" In this way, with every bill that he studies, he calls a member and reproaches him or her by saying, "How do I bring the money for your fees... Why don't you study properly? When will you begin to earn?"

In one of the envelopes is given the information that he has won a lottery worth ten million rupees! But he is not aware of it as he is so tensed up that he fails to see it, even though the envelope is in his hand! He is so busy rebuking everyone that he fails to see that the solution to his problems is in his very hands. Had he known this, would he have been so disturbed? The solution to all his problems had arrived with his problems! On discovering this, his numerous problems would dissolve at once and his tone of speaking to his family members would no longer be the same. There would be love, laughter and contentment in his speech.

Similarly, in spite of happiness lying within him, man lives under severe stress. He sees many problems. He needs to realise that he does not have to solve the problems; he has to learn to dissolve them. This fact may appear far-fetched initially but on delving deep within, you will discover a profound law of life. The next part of this book throws light on this law.

What kind of a letter has reached your hands? What kind of an opportunity has come your way? It is time to recognise it. In the example above, money had come to his rescue and therefore there was no need to get so tensed up. Had he seen the letter conveying the news of the lottery before noticing the bills, wouldn't his tone have been different? Yes, he would have called his son and said, "If you need more money for your books, don't hesitate to ask me." He would have told his wife, "Let there be no dearth of milk at home. Feed the kids to their fill." This reiterates the fact that the solution to every problem already exists, provided we look for the solution first and that would make the problem seem trivial.

Hence it is said, "First things first." If we want to dissolve our problems, then we have to attend to the first thing first. Look at that thing first which is the most important. First know your true self. Basically, that is what spirituality is all about. People feel that they should devote themselves to learning about themselves after fifty years of age. What a great folly it is! This means they would open the envelope containing the cheque of ten million rupees only at the end. Hence it is often stated: "*There is no limit to what ignorance can make us do!*" If we have to dissolve our problems as quickly as possible, then we must realise *who* faces the problem. Then there would be a radical change in our method of solving the problem. Solving problems will then become a joyous affair, a self-expression, an opportunity, making the problem appear as no problem at all. When a problem does not appear to be a problem anymore, then accept that it has been dissolved.

The profound secrets of life help in dissolving our problems. Do not fear problems, but do your homework beforehand. Then learning the art of dissolving problems will not be an ordeal but an exercise to help you stay healthy. *'For the weak, even a small problem is a mountain. For the healthy, even a mountain becomes a molehill.'*

On realising the truth, problems are not solved, but are dissolved immediately

PART 2

Second Supreme Secret of Life

Chapter One

The Second Supreme Secret of Life

How to Live in the Present

The second supreme secret of life says: *Attention on your attention is the greatest meditation. Attention on the greatest meditation is the way to attain God.*

Initially we may find the words difficult and confusing, but soon we will realise that it is all very simple. When can we succeed in focusing our attention on attention? We can't pay attention to our attention by being in the past or the future. We can do it only by being in the present. Whenever we focus on our attention, we *have to* be in the present.

Whatever we focus on grows

Whatever we consistently focus our attention upon grows and blossoms. Till date, what have we focused our attention on? When we give due attention to our children, we find that the children become healthy, grow fast and develop good qualities. It is seen that children who are not given proper attention, try to grab attention from others by breaking or damaging things. They feel that unless and until they don't break something, their parents would not give them attention. When we start giving attention to children in the right proportion, they start growing in the right manner.

Plants on which the gardener devotes his whole-hearted attention automatically grow more than the other plants. Experiments have been conducted in laboratories to prove that plants given attention and those not given attention grow to different heights. Plants which were given more attention developed more than their counterparts which were ignored. Ask yourself what things you give attention to in your life? And once you have understood this secret, what will you do? Decide on what you want in life and start paying attention to those things. If you want good health, you have to focus your attention on health. By doing so, your health will improve spontaneously. The same way, if you pay proper attention to money, then money would multiply.

On grasping this secret, you will pay less attention to negative issues. Let such a time come in your life when your attention does not ever turn to negative things. Till today you may have been pondering over negative thoughts, like 'what if this happens... what if that happens...' This way you are watering the plant of negative thoughts, due to which, wrong things come to thrive in your life. In fact, your focus should never be on negative matters, though the mind habitually does give more attention to negativities. If one tooth is missing, the tongue tends to feel the missing tooth several times in a day. The tongue's attention never goes on the remaining thirty-one teeth. Actually we should focus our attention on things that are available and which we want to grow.

Pay attention to good things that are available in life — it could be your home, your innate qualities, your loyal friends and relatives. Once we start paying attention to the things that we possess, then they start developing. It is human nature that after we receive something we have wanted in life, its importance is lost. Man forgets the value of what he has got; he stops deriving happiness from it. We breathe in air consistently but we are hardly aware of it. Our breathing continues incessantly, but we fail to accept it as a precious gift, because our attention is not on the fact that we have something invaluable — it is because of our breath that we are alive and are able to experience happiness. And the bliss that we can experience through this body that we have received is simply beyond imagination.

Happiness grows by knowing the secrets of life

Due to shortsightedness or lack of knowledge we want to derive happiness from the wrong sources. To derive happiness, some drink alcohol or visit gambling dens or frequent the racecourse. Some others feel, 'Let me get this thing, let me get that thing, let me get a promotion, let this happen, let that happen... then I will be happy.' They are not aware that real happiness lies within them and the way to obtain it is to focus their attention on attention. Understand the secret of where to direct the attention of your attention and then focus at the right place.

On learning where to focus your attention, you will never ever feel any lack of happiness. You won't need to be dependent on others. Today you may be dependent on others, as is obvious when you say, 'This person should praise me, do the task I have assigned, give me a gift on my birthday... then I will be happy. If someone does something for me, then I will get happiness.' But is it not possible that whenever you want and how much you want, you may be able to get from within yourself? Have you come across a person who says, "I am happy because I am alive. To be happy, it is enough that I am. My being is the cause of happiness"? This is possible for each one of us when we realise our true self (self-realisation).

Pay attention to development

To understand the second supreme secret of life, we need to pay attention to our development. Till now we had been focusing our attention on things like, 'How much will be the gain, how much will be the loss?' Just as when a person goes to a discourse, he thinks, 'I am leaving my shop for two hours, what will be my loss? Since I would be away, some of my customers will have to go away.' Think for yourself at what object your attention focuses on more. A time comes in life when we have to rise above profit and loss and give attention to our real (inner) progress. All our life is spent in thinking about profit and loss; this way the real purpose for which we have come to Earth gets lost. Firmly resolve to attend whole-heartedly to those things for which you have been come to this Earth. Work towards achieving that goal, so that some progress is achieved on that front. When we focus our attention on our inner progress, we find that our true development begins. We have to bring about this shift in our life by changing our attention a bit. We are being given information about the House of the Supreme so that we may know the real purpose of life and thereby focus our attention at the right place.

The first window of the House of the Supreme — the past

When we enter the House of the Supreme, then after the floor, we notice the three windows in front of us. We find the word 'past' written on the first window, 'present' on the second window and 'future' on the third window. Let us focus our attention on the second window, which is the most important of all (*see* pictures on the adjacent page).

The first window pertains to the 'past'. We should not pay attention to it as we tend to become what we focus our attention on. Hence we are advised not to pay attention to the past; else we will become the past (a ghost, the one who lives in thoughts only). Learn to live in the present. If we give attention to the truth that is in the present, then we will become the truth. Let the past be kept closed; let the curtains remain drawn on that window. In spite of telling this, people tend to get entangled in illusion (*maya*), in delusion, in the mirage of an illusory world and the window to the past. This is because on the inside of this window, a very realistic picture of a beautiful scenery is stuck. Looking at it, you feel that there is a garden outside from which you can get a lot of fresh air and oxygen. Due to this reason you open the window, draw the curtains aside and take long breaths (i.e. delve deep in the past). But later you realise that due to opening this window, you are feeling choked. Actually, that window is a closed window. From that window you can never get any air. By standing in front of a closed window, our life is ruined. We begin to live like a corpse.

Many people come to know only when they are dying that they did not live life at all. People spend their entire life living in the past. They never live where they ought to live. In reality, our true life is in the present, oxygen is in the present, but you want to get oxygen from the past and take deep breaths due to which you get a heart attack (hate attack). Past incidents arouse hatred and guilt such as, 'Why did this happen with me? Why did he do that? Why did I do so in my unconsciousness?' You have to get liberated from both, the past and the future. You have to be liberated from guilt and hatred. You should be aware as to which window does not need to be opened, even if the most attractive scene is seen through that window.

The third window — the future

The third window is that of the 'future', which is closed. It is locked with a huge padlock. In the centre of the lock is the hole for inserting the key. This hole runs across the entire breadth of the lock. But we feel that this hole traverses even the window. We think that we can get fresh air from outside through this hole in the lock. From the lock of the window of the 'future' we can never get any fresh air. This is a blunder on our part. Similarly, we search for a cure to our miseries in the future, forgetting the fact that a beautiful future can be created only in the present. Some people build castles in the air and keep somersaulting in their imagination of the future. As a result of this, their present also slips away. Work that needs to be done today is left undone. Thus they get trapped in a net of disillusionment and stress.

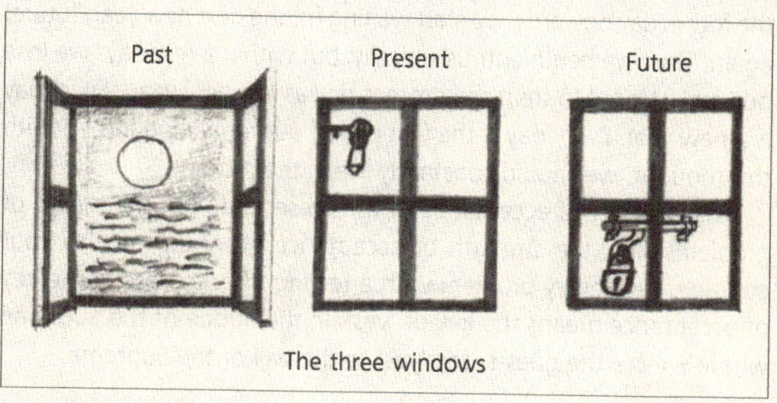

The three windows

Students do not study in the present due to which they face extreme stress during their examinations. Out of stress, some are even forced to commit suicide.

Without attending to his work, a person whiles away time in backbiting, gossiping and criticising others in office. This way he becomes an enemy of his own future. Those who do a good job in their present get promoted in their field. The key to a bright future lies in the present moment.

The window of the present

Between the windows of the 'past' and the 'future' lies one more window, called the window of the 'present'. A key hangs at the window, and by using it, the lock to the future can be opened.

But what happens is that we commit the mistake of searching for the key to the lock of the future window on the 'future' window itself, i.e. we keep wading in thoughts of the future. Leaving the present aside, we search for the key to the future. We need to realise that the key to the future is kept at the window of the 'present'. The one who looks for the key in the present will find it and the second supreme secret of life will unveil before him.

After learning about the second supreme secret of life, your life will become new, bright and fresh. Whenever a new year begins, we all feel very enthused. We make all kinds of resolutions on that day, saying that we will do this and do that. We try to do many new things, but soon the enthusiasm wanes in two to three days and from the fourth day onwards, we start waiting for the next new year (future) again. Thus we begin enthusiastically, but within a few days we lose our zeal. We fail to treat the present day as the new year. 'Every day is a new year. Every day is the first day of our remaining life' — with this thought, we should constantly live in the present.

Use the key of acceptance of the present; do not get scared of problems. Test the strength of acceptance every day as also your courage. Face every problem with a feeling of acceptance. The key of acceptance means the key of 'yes'. In the abode of the Supreme where we are the guests, say 'yes' to the will of the Supreme.

The present is alive, the rest is just ash

In the present moment, let us find liberation from the black day and white night. 'Black day' means 'black ash'. Black ash means unpleasant but dead memories of the past. 'White night' means 'white ash', which includes pleasant dead memories of the past. Both these memories are ash. Everyone wants to get rid of 'black ash', but not the 'white ash'. But we fail to realise that even 'white ash' spoils our present. We tend to recall and relive and re-experience the old pleasures during moments of happiness that we get in the present. We say, 'Last Christmas was better…we enjoyed more during last year's holiday; this year is not much fun…we were happier when we were young…'By entertaining such thoughts, we spoil the happiness of the present.

By standing in front of the window of the 'past', the unpleasant memories (black ash) bring back the guilt, the tears and the repentance. Whatever be the colour of ash, ash is ash. In ash, there are only bones. There is nothing alive in it; there is no spark, no consciousness in it. The present is alive; it is now, it is here, it is consciousness. Learn to live in the present. By living in the present, our unconsciousness (mechanical existence) breaks. Rising above a mechanical life, let us become new and alive in the present. In this new life, allow new decisions, new skills, new activities, new habits, new routines, new books, new friends and new thoughts to enter. This entry is possible only through the window of the 'present'.

A person searches for a remedy to his miseries in the future and his happiness in memories of the past. He does not have the knowledge that the creation of a beautiful future and experience of bliss is possible only in the present.

Chapter Two

THE GREATEST MEDITATION

WISDOM LIES IN GETTING LIBERATED FROM PAST AND FUTURE

'*Attention on attention is the greatest meditation.*' Such meditation is possible only in the present. When we focus our attention on the present, people tend to ask, "Are you meditating?" Our reply is, "No, I am paying attention to my attention." Understand that this statement is beyond most people. To understand this, we need to learn how to pay attention to our attention by practising the meditation given below. After meditating for a few minutes, we will learn its secret and what witness and self-witness are.

After reading all the instructions given below, you can immediately start practising this meditation.

Attention on attention — an exercise

- In the practice of meditation, sit in a relaxed posture. Then look at the scene around you. You may have seen the picture earlier, you are seeing it now and you will see it in the future too. But what will be the difference? Till now, whenever you saw the scene, due to your habit you never looked at it intently, because your mind had already predetermined that you knew it and 'I know its name. This is a clock, this is a wall, this is a window, this is a curtain, this is a button, this is a fan...' But in this exercise, you should not view things in the same manner as your eyes looked at the surroundings and objects earlier. In this meditation, your manner of viewing things will undergo a change.

- Look at things around you as if you do not know the name of anything. While doing this form of meditation, you will realise that your style of viewing undergoes a change. This is because when an object is given a name (label), you stop seeing it. When you remove the label attached to an object, you truly begin to see it.
- For any object, if you were to say, 'I don't know the name of this article,' you will be able to see it minutely and feel amazed at the sight. Through this exercise, you will see each entity like a child. A child is able to see each object very distinctly, with great interest and joy, because the child does not know the name of the object. Hence it is said that spirituality is about becoming a child again; to learn to be amazed again. Bring this amazement and joy into your life at once and do not delay or wait for fifty years to pass.
- After fully looking at one object, look at the second and then the third. Look at it as though you are not aware of its name. Look at every object and say, 'I don't know what this object is. I only know that I don't know'. This is called the state of 'bright (*tej*) ignorance', which means, *'I know that I don't know.'* This is the state in which you need to carry out this meditation. Find who are the people around you — a boy or a girl? You do not know. Carry out this entire meditation with the attitude of not knowing the identity of anything.
- While looking at a scene, pay attention to that on which your attention is, from where it slips, from where it gets scattered and where it gets entangled. Knowing all these aspects about your attention is 'attention on attention'.
- After completing the 'open eye' meditation, close your eyes

and feel the environment all around you. Is it cold or hot, is there stiffness or lightness in your legs, is your body tired or sleepy? Feel these things.

- Now open your eyes and look at your body, your hands but do not say, 'This is my hand.' Instead ask, 'What object is this? I don't know what it is.' Only then will you be able to see your body without attachment.
- Close your eyes and feel the detachment towards your body. Feel that you are *with* the body and not the body. You are '*with* the body' means that you are 'a companion of the body'. Observe every sensation that arises in your body with detachment. Apply the same approach to your sensations and say, 'What this sensation is, I do not know.'
- Now with eyes closed listen to all the sounds that are present around you. Recognise all the different sounds but do not get stuck on any one sound. Try to detect even the subtlest of sounds. After knowing one sound, move on and try to listen to the next.
- While meditating with eyes closed, observe where your attention gets stuck, from where it slips and where it simply fails to stay.
- With eyes closed, focus your attention on thoughts present within you. At that moment, what are the thoughts that are going on? Without labelling them as good or bad, just watch them pass by. Have the thoughts stopped appearing or has a thought appeared which says to you, 'There is no thought now'. Learn this.

Remain in this state for two minutes and then open your eyes. You will feel fresh after doing this meditation. What is your attention? Where does it drift? Which objects does it get attracted to and slip away from? In which thoughts does it get stuck? Which thoughts does it chase? Which thoughts does it let go? In which thoughts does it get entangled? You will know all this through meditation while learning to pay attention to your attention, which is very important.

Through meditation your thoughts get the right direction. Aimless thoughts that keep appearing without any rhyme or reason, will automatically stop. This will improve your concentration and help you notice those subtle things about yourself that you were earlier unaware of.

The open window of the present

Meditation on the present is such a window that provides you with oxygen. The word 'now' is written on it. 'Now' is where there is no tomorrow and no yesterday. The window of *now,* the window of the present, is liberation from yesterday which has gone and the liberation from tomorrow that is yet to come. It is liberation from misery. At this window is hung the key to the future. If in the present you analyse what mistakes you have made and what you have learnt from them, then you would be able to make good use of the past. Your mistakes will get corrected and your future will improve and be bright. The past and future can be made use of only in the present. Only if right work is done in the present will your future be reformed.

After using the past to learn from your mistakes, the past needs to be discarded, just as the refill of a pen is discarded after use. After learning and improving on your past mistakes, bury the past in a coffin because, 'the past is not BAD; it is DEAD.'

Attain liberation from strife of the past and future and become the witness of self-witness

'One who is liberated from the past and future has his work done through wisdom.' You need to work on the window of '*now*'. You have to focus your attention on the present. Be a witness to whatever is happening in the present. Witnessing the witness is to become a self-witness. Hence it is called 'meditating on meditation' and is the missing link in spirituality. All over the world many people meditate, but they get entangled only in the benefits of meditation. Agreed, the benefits are important but do not stop there. There is also a step further the understanding of which is very crucial.

Becoming a witness to 'witness' means the 'return of meditation to the source from whence it emanates'. It then becomes self-meditation and there remains no obstacle. That is the way to attain God. Only on becoming a witness to the witness does real meditation begin. Until we are aware of 'who am I?' (the true self), we cannot know how to witness the witness. When we do the 'who am I?' meditation or 'complete meditation', we gradually return to our true self and experience the state of *samadhi*. It is then that we understand what is meant by 'being witness of the witness' (self-witness). During sleep we are in the experience of the self-witness, but there is no witness in that state. When we experience that state in a wakeful state, we become self-witness. Self-witness is the final state.

Awareness about attention will bring about revolutionary changes in us. Those who have already been practising meditation can take it to the next level.

If in the present, you can reflect on what mistake you made in the past and how you would do it differently in the future, only then will your future be reformed and become bright. One who is liberated from the past and future gets his work done through wisdom.

Chapter Three

The Art of Living in the Present

The One-handed Snap or Clap

We go to see a play. There are several artistes on the stage and our favourite teacher is seen playing a role too. There are many teachers in school whom we have liked, and for whom we have had great respect. One among them is seen playing a negative role in the play. While deeply immersed in the play being staged, we get very angry with the one playing the negative role. But when we recall that our teacher is only enacting a role, our anger evaporates.

However, we often forget this while watching the play; hence we have to be reminded each time that this is the same teacher for whom we have great respect. On remembering this, our anger disappears. Then we do not get too involved in the play or get stuck to the role.

A boy named Tinu, frustrated with life, ran off to the forest. There a sage solved his problem and gave him supernatural power. The sage told him, "Whenever you snap your fingers, you will move on to the next scene of your life. Due to this you will never be frustrated in your life. Whenever you feel frustrated, snap your fingers and the next scene will appear before you."

On receiving the occult power, a delighted Tinu returned home.

When he sat down to do his studies at home, he began to get bored. Hence, he snapped his fingers and the next scene appeared before him. In this scene he appeared sitting for his exams. He found this scene also troublesome and so he snapped his fingers again. The next scene appeared wherein he saw himself in the higher class and studying. The teacher was teaching him mathematics. He again got bored with mathematics and snapped his fingers. The next scene appeared. Continuing this way, he came to the scene of finding himself working in an office. There too his boss began to scold him and so he immediately snapped his fingers and saw his wedding ceremony. He liked this scene, but in his enthusiasm to see which good scene lay ahead, he snapped his fingers again. He found himself playing with his children. He liked this scene very much too. Everything was going on well, but after a few days he got bored. He snapped his fingers again and saw his children getting married. Ultimately he came to the scene when he becomes an old man. When death draws near, he realises, 'Due to this occult power, I didn't live at all. Wherever I was, I always kept running ahead from there. Whatever was happening in the present, I did not live it at all.'

The signal of coming to the present

If by snapping your fingers, you reached the next scene, then by clapping the one-handed clap you can return to the present. The one-handed clap is made by joining the thumb and the index finger and cannot be heard by others. It is audible only to you. By the one-handed clap, the experiencer experiences the experience in the experience, i.e. the viewer himself becomes the seen and sees himself. If there is just one hand, then how will the clap take place? As there is just one self, there is nothing else other than the self in the universe and beyond. Then who will see what? (The fact is that the self created this world; it created different objects and different beings out of itself, so that it could see itself). Whenever you find that you are getting entangled in either the past or the future scenes, join the thumb and the index finger and tell yourself, 'Dear! Come back to the present.'

Once, in the court of famous Emperor Akbar, who ruled over

India, another king sent two flowers and asked the question, "Which of the two is a real flower?" The answer had to be given without touching or smelling the flowers. All the courtiers thought over this question, but no one could think of an answer. Then Akbar turned to Birbal and asked him the same question. Birbal was very well known for his intelligence and wisdom; he served as a minister in the court of Emperor Akbar. Birbal replied, "The answer is very simple. Just open all the windows of the court."

On opening the windows, some honeybees flew in and settled on one of the flowers. Birbal said, "This is the real flower."

From this it becomes clear that on opening the window of the present (wisdom), there is the possibility of taking the right decisions.

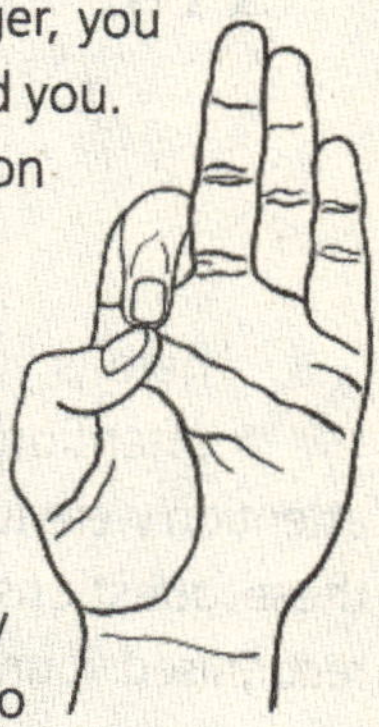

Whenever you join your thumb and index finger, you come to the present and begin to see things around you. In this manner, your exercise of attention on attention begins. If you do this meditation for even a few moments, you will become free from thoughts and thus be able to do fresh and bright deeds. By getting entangled in the past or future thoughts, there is a possibility of taking wrong decisions. Snapping the fingers, you used to enter the future. Now by performing the one-handed clap, you can come to the present.

You have understood the second secret — learn to live in the present by performing the one-handed clap.

Chapter Four

The Basic Aim of Meditation

Do not get Entangled in Benefits

Where is your attention? When will your attention return to attention? How can you do complete meditation? When attention were to reach attention, how will your life be? Contemplate these questions. When you begin to live your life after having recognised your true self, then it will make no difference to you as to how other people live or what is of importance to them. You will act only upon your own conviction and faith. You will live, knowing and recognising yourself.

Taste meditation all through life

Millions of people are waiting for someone to begin meditating before they begin to do so. No one begins and hence they too do not do it. We do not know that they wait for us while we wait for them. When a force arrives that drives man to meditate, then because of the force he gets the taste of meditation. After tasting it once, he wants to taste it all his life.

Through various practices we wish to experience the state of *samadhi*. Some meditate and some do not. Those who meditate make true progress. In meditation, getting results or answers is not as important. What is important is to meditate and give the mind the practice to concentrate (focus). Through continuous practice, the mind develops the habit of concentration, contemplation and prayer.

Before prayer

A beginner in meditation is given to recite some prayer. The feeling by praying should be such that he experiences the same feeling as that of sitting in a temple with hands folded together in reverence. This takes him into the depth of meditation. Before offering a prayer, another prayer is recited in order to make the prayer effective. Recite the following prayer before offering your prayer:

'The prayer that I am going to offer now is going to have the best effect on my body and mind.' This prayer is the 'bright (*tej*) prayer' before our prayer. Begin with this bright prayer and then say the actual prayer. Keep the happy thought in mind that may God liberate you from identification and attachment with desires. In this manner you reach that state where the ego dissolves, where wisdom awakens and the experiencer experiences the experience in experience. Only meditation remains and the meditator (the individual who thinks himself to be a separate entity) disappears. The one who begins meditation, the one who says, "I will meditate" disappears in that state. In this journey, bliss is attained only on losing yourself and your ego.

Till today we have been deriving happiness by protecting our ego. But the joy we get from meditation is several times greater. The happiness of serving our ego is nothing in comparison to the greatest meditation. Man has not experimented this before and hence had always wanted to derive happiness by protecting his ego.

Basic purpose

Ego always wants that whenever the experience, the self-realisation, the glimpse of God, occurs, it should be present. But it is not aware that if it is present, then there will be no self-experience (glimpse of God). Only one among the two can be present, i.e. either our true self or our ego (false self). Only when you understand this, does the surrender of your ego take place, and you reach the state of *samadhi*.

Some call this state as *samadhi* while others call it Divine devotion (*bhakti*). All these words are only to take you towards God. Every technique has its advantages. Every practice is a path, i.e. it takes you ahead. Due to the meditation technique, you derive some other benefits too which can be termed as bonus. As your concentration increases, many of your tasks also get accomplished. Your body becomes ready to become a medium of self-expression, but your aim is not to get entangled in these benefits. You have to remember the basic purpose of meditation — to attain that experience which is called self-witness, attention on attention, experience of the self or complete self-realisation.

Take each step to reach complete meditation

Those whose level of consciousness is low are helped to raise it. In other words, for those who lie deep in the well, a ladder of understanding is sent from a helicopter so that they can emerge from the well. When the ladder appears, the person in the well raises his head. This means that his level of consciousness goes up. Otherwise by remaining in the well, his level of consciousness can never rise. It is to raise the level of consciousness that help is given in the form of a ladder (knowledge). But if we mistake that ladder to be a snake, then we will never be able to benefit from it. When we consider the ladder to be a ladder and not a snake, then everything coming from above will help us, even if it is a snake. That snake too will do the job of a ladder for us. If we have recognised the truth, then we will be able to take full advantage of everything that appears in life. Thus moving ahead, step by step, we will be able to perform complete meditation. This will get accomplished by putting every piece together. However, before that, we need to understand meditation completely. If we meditate with understanding, we will be able to take full advantage of it.

Chapter Five

Unconsciousness in Sleep, Awareness in *Samadhi*

Centre Balancing Meditation

We all sleep at night but we enter the sleep state without understanding. After sleeping for eight hours, we wake up in the morning, feeling the same as we were earlier, and many a time, we wake up feeling worse than before by not getting proper sleep — backache, swelling of the eyes or having unpleasant dreams. When we sleep, it means we go into the experience of the self. Waking up from sleep means coming out of that experience. Sleep is also a kind of *samadhi*, but what is the difference when we sleep and when we enter *samadhi*? Let us understand this difference.

When we enter the sleep state, we actually enter the state of unconsciousness while when we go into *samadhi,* we enter into consciousness. Only after waking up in the morning do we realise that we were asleep. In *samadhi*, we are aware that we are going into *samadhi*. In this state, there is just knowing and the knower (the consciousness) is being known. The viewer (seer) witnesses himself, i.e. the one who sees becomes the 'seen' for himself. Understand this through the following example.

You stand in front of a mirror. At that time, you are the knower and in that mirror you know your own self. This means that you are the viewer as well as the seen, and it is you who is seeing. Initially, you consider the viewer and the seen as separate (*see* picture). But later both become one. When the viewer, the seen and the act of seeing (witnessing) become one, then the phenomenon of *samadhi* occurs.

Otherwise, we know that the subject, the object and the action are three separate entities. *Samadhi* is the state where the viewer, the seeing and the seen become one. Then, we see all the objects in the world from the state of being one. We alone are the viewer, the seeing and the seen. In this way, the secret of Trinity (the three) unfolds before us.

Samadhi is the only state where the three are one. This state is also called the state of witnessing (*darshan*) or self-witness.

In sleep there is ignorance and in *samadhi*, there is understanding

Samadhi and sleep are similar states. Often, while practising meditation, people drift into sleep and don't even realise it. Only when someone awakens them, do they realise that they were in sleep. You go into sleep due to lethargy, dullness or fatigue. In sleep, along with unconsciousness, there is ignorance. However, in *samadhi* there is complete consciousness. The most important thing is you should enter the state of *samadhi* with understanding. The mind of man is a cage of beliefs and understanding is the key. Also, you need to go into *samadhi* with freshness, a feeling of acceptance and freedom from desire.

In the state of *samadhi*, there is no mind which keeps checking, 'Is this happening or not? Why am I not getting the same experience today that I got yesterday?' Whether you get a similar experience or not, you must continue the meditation and go into *samadhi* free from such desires. During meditation, whether some things are acceptable or not, whether you get the desired results or not, only your presence is important. Continue the practice with unceasing regularity and keep going into *samadhi*. Where the feeling of acceptance, understanding and knowledge are present, unconsciousness and ignorance do not exist. From this you would have understood what is the difference between going into *samadhi* and going into sleep.

Be in touch with *tejasthan*

We develop the conviction about our true nature in *samadhi*. In the state of *samadhi*, we are on our *tejasthan*. By repeatedly going into *samadhi,* we need to obtain a knack by which we can be in touch with the *tejasthan* all the time, even while carrying on daily routines, like interacting with people or while working. *Tejasthan* literally translates into 'the bright place'. *Tejasthan* actually means that place where the self is connected with the body, where the formless and the form unite, where the union (*yog*) takes place. It can be grossly considered in the area of the heart. Let a part of our mind always remain in that area, in that state of self-meditation.

In the game, pay attention to both the *tejasthan* and the *maya* (illusion)

Let us understand the state of *samadhi* through an analogy. We play a game in which there are two teams. One team is on our side and the other team is opposite to us. The players in my team hold each other's hands, one behind the other. One player holds my hand. Likewise, the opposite players also hold each other's hands. Now both teams try to pull each other towards themselves. This game is similar to the tug-of-war, where people on both sides pull at the opposite ends of a rope towards themselves. In exactly the same way, we clutch the hand of the opponent. People from my team pull me behind and the people from the opposite team pull me ahead. If our strength is superior, we don't get entangled in the opposite team. But if our strength is less or we turn out to be weaker, we land up in the opposite team. Our team is that of *tejasthan* and the opposite team is that of illusion or *maya*.

In this game, our attention will be on the hand and strength of the opponent as also on our teammate pulling us from behind. Our attention is on both sides. In other words, one portion of our mind is on the *tejasthan* and the other on the illusion in front of us.

Train your attention

If your attention is on the *tejasthan,* then you can win the game. If you realise the truth and understand your true self, you will definitely win. However, if you focus only on illusion, you will land up in illusion. Attention is a double-ended arrow, which flies both ways. Only when our attention is on both sides, can we work in this world by remaining detached from the illusion just as the lotus blooms fresh in muddy waters. Even if water is sprinkled on it, the water slides off. Similarly, if we want to prevent the illusion from affecting us even while living in this illusory world, we must train our attention.

As soon as we enter this illusory world, we need to remember the *mantra*, *'Turn around! Where is your attention?'* Our attention should not only be in front, but also behind. Only then can we win this game between illusion and truth. When we forget this game, we get too entangled in it. We see something negative in the opposite person and begin to act like him due to ignorance. When we get the art of focusing correctly, we see only what we want to see in the opposite person. We have to make up our mind on what we want.

See virtue in everyone

We go to a party and find everyone seated at his place with his plate in front. A glance at their plates tells us what dishes are being served. We focus our attention only on those dishes which we desire to eat. In the matter of food our focus is sharp, then why can't we sharpen our focus in the matter of virtue? Focus only on those qualities of others which you want to imbibe.

In the first step of meditation, you have to clean and purify your mind. See only that which you want to possess. Do you see ego or divine devotion in the people you meet? Just as the food you eat affects you, so also what you see in others affects you.

If someone vomits what he has eaten, then would you like to eat the same food that he had taken? If we pay careful attention to whatever is visible in the world, we will notice that some things cause trouble and some things bring peace in life. We should not consume food that makes us belch and produces bad odour. We need to consume only those foods, which spread a pleasant aroma, encourage good health and make the face radiant and bright. We get the opportunity to see everything and be with all kinds of people. Some people are ahead of us while others are coming ahead looking at us. All kinds of arrangements have been made in this world for us.

Train your eyes, ears and tongue

Along with our attention, our eyes, ears and tongue too need to be trained first. We must pay attention to what our eyes look at and what our ears hear. If someone backbites, speaks ill of others and indulges in worthless chatter, then we should confirm whether that is what our ears want to hear. In this manner, we would always pay attention to our eyes and ears.

Also we need to pay attention to what our tongue wants to speak. If the tongue does not utter the name of God, then the tongue is useless. If the ears do not listen to the discourses on truth, then the ears are useless. If the eyes do not witness the self-witness, then the eyes are a waste. If our attention does not focus on attention, then attention is no good. Once we are convinced about this, we would try to take advantage of every single moment of all the arrangements made in this world.

Pay attention to attention

First the eyes and ears have to be trained, then the tongue. As long as we do not pay attention to smell, the nose does not bother us much. However, the two main senses, namely the eyes and the ears, keep drawing our attention from morning till night. We do not bother to think, 'Where is my eye going? What am I seeing? I ought to pay attention to this too.' Similarly, we need to pay attention to our attention. We have to decide what should be the focus of our attention from morning to night. Till today we had never asked ourselves about where our attention was focused and hence it wandered everywhere. But from now on, let our attention go anywhere only after receiving our permission. Ask it, 'Where are you going? Turn around! Where is your attention?' When we ask this, our attention starts getting trained. The happiness and benefits we derive from this will be enormous.

Centre-balancing meditation

'Centre-balancing meditation' means aligning our body in accordance with the gravitational force of the Earth, so that we may sit in actual meditation for a longer period of time and delve into the depths of meditation. Before practising any meditation technique, the manner of sitting and the posture of the body are important. Hence this meditation should be done before every meditation. Whenever we sit, our body posture should be in accordance with the gravitational force of the Earth. If we follow this rule, then we can sit for a longer time without any discomfort. But how can we know whether we are sitting in alignment with the gravitational force or not? How do we know where the centre of our body is? It is precisely for this reason that this meditation is done.

Let us understand through an example how to find the centre of our body. When we make a pen stand in an upright position on a table, how is it able to stand? This is because it has found its centre. Its centre is correctly aligned with the force of gravity. If we keep the pencil tilted, we will find that its centre is not properly aligned and it will no longer be able to stand in this position. In a similar manner, when our body is positioned at its centre, then it will remain steady for a longer period of time. If we place our body in a wrong posture, after a short duration it will begin to experience pain, and we will not be able to sit for long. However, the body has a centre point, which is equivalent to a needle point. If we sit in such a posture we will be able to sit for hours together without feeling tired.

Procedure for the centre-balancing meditation

- Stand at one place.
- Keep some distance between the feet (about 6 inches).
- Keeping the feet steady, push the upper body or torso forward and ask yourself, 'If I keep my body in this posture, will I feel tired?' The answer will be, 'Yes, you will definitely feel tired.'
- Balancing your feet, move your upper body backwards, and again ask the same question. In which position (in between forward and backward) will you be able to stand for a longer period of time without getting tired?
- Again keeping your feet steady, move your body forward and backward like a pendulum. Just like the pendulum returns to its position on its own, reduce your forward and backward body movements, until you reach the centre.
- A point will be reached when you can discover that you can neither go forward nor backward. This is the only point where you can remain stable.
- Now you need to move left and right. This also needs to be done in the same manner as described above (you have to move left and right like a pendulum).
- From these four directions, you can identify your centre point. Remain in this position and enjoy it.
- Sit in the meditation posture and repeat all the steps given above to locate your centre in the sitting position.

Additional benefits of this exercise

- In case you are in a situation where everybody around is under stress and there is a conflict going on, you can begin this experiment with the thought, 'I am able to balance myself in this situation.' If your body is balanced, then it can have a similar effect on the mental plane too.
- If in any situation or event, you feel that you are getting out of control, by maintaining your physical balance, you can also balance all the other planes.

Chapter Six

Preparation Before Meditation

Twelve Things to Do Before Meditation

Practise meditation either in the morning or evening

Meditate either in the morning or evening, as it has been considered the ideal time for meditation. Of the two, morning is more beneficial because there is less dust in the atmosphere in comparison to the evening. Since people keep walking the streets throughout the day, the dust keeps rising and spreading in the atmosphere. In fact, the whole atmosphere is full of dust, though this is not apparent. Morning time is better than the evening time because people sleep at night and hence the dust settles down before the break of dawn. The morning atmosphere is beneficial for *pranayama* (breath control exercise) too. Inhalation of fresh air in a pure environment is twice as beneficial. Hence, morning time is considered ideal for meditation and *pranayama*.

In the early morning hours, we are neither fully awake nor fully asleep. We are in a state where the frequency of the brain is low. This state is known as the 'alpha state', which is a relaxed state. Nature prepares and presents us such an atmosphere in the morning, hence the morning hours are considered an ideal environment for meditation. Along with morning, the evening time is also chosen for meditation because after working throughout the day, we are tired and want to sleep. In such a state, the frequency of the brain is again low.

Attend to your activities slowly before meditation

A person is constantly on his feet throughout the day and hence his brain is very active. Meditation requires that we should work slowly. Therefore we are advised to slow down our activities before meditation. If we are going to sit in meditation ten minutes later, then we should slow down our activities for the next ten minutes. If going to the wash-basin, we should proceed slowly and wash our face slowly. If we have to lift something to sit upon, we should keep it down slowly. Rest of the time we lift things up hurriedly and place them here and there, but we have to avoid doing so before meditation.

Prepare body and mind before meditation

While meditating, we enter within, hence it is essential to bring our body into the state of meditation before commencing meditation. We also need to prepare ourselves mentally before meditation. Tell your mind before you begin, 'I was in a hurry earlier, but now I am going to do everything slowly.' Prior to meditation, carry out your tasks slowly for some time and prepare your seating arrangement for meditation slowly so as to be ready for meditation. By your behaviour, other people will also come to know that you are meditating. You are slowing down your pace because you are going to enter into meditation, it means you are going to do nothing (meditation is 'doing nothing'). If you have to do something, then speed would be essential.

Practise meditation on an empty stomach

At night, food gets digested and the stomach becomes empty in the morning. This helps in meditating. In the evening, lunch gets digested and meditation can be done better on an empty stomach.

Benefits from the special environment while meditating

In the morning, after freshening yourself and taking a bath, wear loose clothes or clothes that will not bother you during meditation. If we sit in front of a plain wall of our house for meditation, it will prove helpful as it would curb visual distractions even if we happen to open our eyes during meditation. If we are lucky enough to meditate in a natural environment, we must certainly derive benefit from it. Many a times, Nature helps in awakening the internal nature.

Switch off the telephone while meditating

Before sitting for meditation, ensure that the cell phone or telephones do not ring during meditation. If there is a possibility of the phone ringing, switch it off. Take care that you are not disturbed during meditation.

Meditate in peaceful surroundings

While meditating, if people around you sit and chat, your attention will be diverted towards their conversation. This would be just like a stork that stands still on one leg in water, but its attention is on the fish swimming below. One who sees the stork will feel that it is meditating, but actually it is searching for its food. Similarly, while meditating, if people around you talk, your attention will go towards their conversation. 'Are they saying something which is useful for me? Are they saying anything good or bad about me?' Such thoughts will bother you. Never meditate in such a surrounding.

Always use the same seat for meditation

When meditating every day at the same time, same place, on the same seat, in the same posture, with the same technique and the same type of meditation, the body automatically gets ready as it becomes conditioned to the routine. On reaching the destined spot, your body gets ready instantly, your thoughts slow down and you are able to watch your thoughts since your focus is on meditating and nothing else. The seat that you use for meditation must be kept apart from other furniture. Do not sit casually on it and do not watch television by sitting on this seat, because the effect of the seat will get reduced or vanish. By using the same seat, you mentally prepare yourself at once.

On waking up in the morning, you need not put in much effort to brush your teeth, to become fresh and take a bath. The body immediately gets ready because it knows that after waking up, these particular activities have to be done. The body gets habituated to this daily routine in the morning. Likewise, you have to develop a habit with the meditation seat. After sitting on this seat, you should not pursue any thought but just meditate. You may get very nice thoughts or great ideas, but sitting on that seat, you should not run after such thoughts. At that time, since you are seated for meditation, all you have to do is to meditate.

The importance of *mudra* in meditation

While always adopt the same *mudra* (symbolic hand gesture; particular placement of the palms and fingers). There are several benefits of this. The *mudras* designed for meditation are meant to help you. When you reach the depths of meditation, you can make the *mudra* as you like, either with one hand or with both hands. While meditating, you can make the *mudra* with one hand so that you can go into the state of meditation even while walking, writing or doing any other work. While carrying out your worldly chores, if bothered by worries, or if stressed out either due to exams or something else, you can use this *mudra*. When you are in a state of stress or worry, and if you join your thumb and the index finger (or any *mudra* that you use while meditating), then immediately the same meditative state will be produced in your body. The body does not know whether it is in the interview hall or on the stage or anywhere else. When you adopt the meditation *mudra*, the body gets the intimation that you are ready for meditation and will immediately feel peaceful, as if in a state of meditation. In this state you are able to recollect the forgotten things and forget about worry and tension.

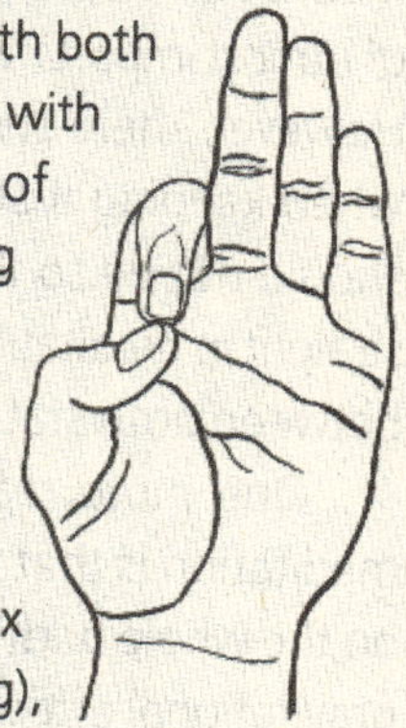

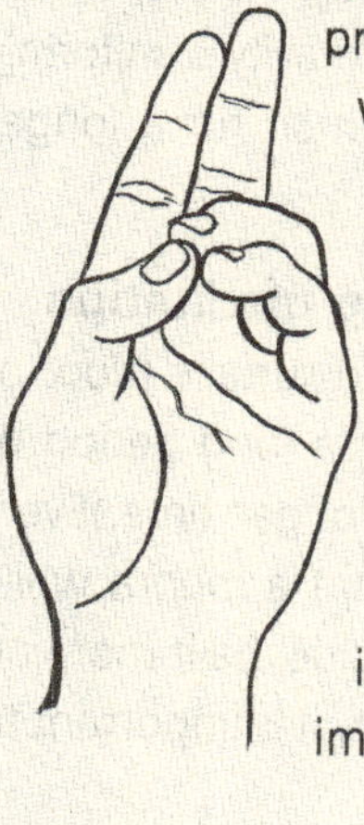

You can take advantage of this *mudra* even in taking decisions. Every *mudra* has its own importance. When you adopt a *mudra*, certain acupressure points get pressed which prove helpful in improving your health.

While meditating, you have to sit on the same seat each time and your second seat is your own body. You have to prepare yourself to such an extent that your own body becomes the seat of meditation. When your body becomes the seat, then in future, whenever you want to lower the frequency of the brain or calm it down, just by adopting the *mudra* you can calm down instantly and reach greater depths.

Keep the backbone straight in meditation

The backbone is of the greatest importance in the body's posture during meditation. Those who want to do a lot of work on the path of meditation or those who want to attain perfection in meditation, it is of utmost importance to keep the backbone straight during meditation. However, there should not be too much tension on the backbone when keeping it straight for meditation. Conversely, the backbone should not be so totally relaxed that it bends during meditation. Sit straight in meditation and relax the backbone a little to strike a balance between both states.

One more reason for keeping the backbone straight during meditation is that the gravitational force of the Earth acts uniformly on the whole body in this posture and hence no pain is felt. When the gravitational effect is greater on some parts and lesser on other parts of the body, pain may be experienced in the body. Hence, find a point or a posture for the body wherein the effect of gravity is uniformly spread all over the body. In such a state you can sit for a longer period without getting tired.

Choose a suitable seat for the body during meditation

For meditation, you can spread a carpet on a hard surface (floor or ground). If you cannot sit on a hard surface for a long period of time, choose a seat on which you can sit for a longer time. Every person has to choose a seat that suits him. Adopt a *mudra* while meditating and benefit from it. Be it inside or outside, be it morning or evening, be it in front of a wall or amidst Nature, it is important to meditate every day at the same time. Whether people are around you or not, you have to meditate attentively. If the talks of those around you interest you, your attention gets diverted. Hence when you are a beginner, quiet surroundings (maybe a Silence Room) can be of great help.

On attaining perfection in meditation, you will find it as easy as riding a bicycle. When you become an expert in riding a bicycle, then you can ride it under every circumstance. Even if your dress is tight, you can ride it. On a crowded street, in the bazaar, anywhere, you will have no problem riding it. The same is the case with meditation. When you become an expert, you will be able to meditate anywhere and in any condition.

Sit at least for twenty minutes in meditation

Initially during meditation, a number of varied thoughts may arise within you. However, when you meditate regularly, then after sitting for meditation the thoughts will disappear very soon. You would no longer need to sit for a longer duration in meditation.

In order to reach such a state, it is recommended that in the begining you must sit in meditation for twenty minutes at least. This is because out of the twenty minutes, the first five to seven minutes get spent in calming down the thoughts. In the last five minutes, you will begin to ask yourself, 'Is it time or not? Now I have to get up.' In between all this, you actually get only five or six minutes for meditation. Hence the duration of at least twenty minutes is recommended. Subsequently over time, the duration of meditation increases on its own.

Those who have less time or have to go out, can set a buzzer. People have the fear that if they go into *samadhi*, instead of twenty minutes, an hour also may elapse due to unawareness of time. Their work would then get delayed. The solution is to set a timer. While meditating, if we keep checking the watch again and again, we cannot enter into deep meditation. Those who look at the watch repeatedly feel as if a long time has passed in meditation, although only five minutes may have elapsed. On the other hand, many a times, people feel that only a short time has passed, when actually an hour could have passed. This way different types of states are experienced, making the use of the buzzer effective.

Chapter Seven

Complete Meditation

Who am I?

Complete meditation is essential for every person just as taking a daily bath is. By meditating daily, our mind's slate gets cleansed. By filling the mind with thoughts and failing to cleanse the slate, stress builds up. Meditation liberates us from stress and gives us the bliss of self-realisation. Begin this meditation by following the procedure given below. First read this chapter again and again and imbibe the procedure. You can also record all the instructions sequentially on a tape and then meditate according to the instructions imparted by playing the tape. You have to keep your eyes closed throughout this meditation.

- Close your eyes and sit in meditation posture (*sukhasana* or any convenient posture) with a *mudra* (*dhyan mudra* or any other preferred *mudra, see* picture on p. 101).
- Keeping the body steady, listen to all the sounds around you. Identify at least five different sounds, but don't be in a hurry. With a quiet mind, focus your attention on various sounds and move on to the next sound. Don't get stuck with a particular sound and start listening only to that. Just identify the sound and move ahead.

- If there is a sound of the rotating fan, then there are other subtle sounds produced within that sound too. Listen to them attentively. Various types of sounds can include conversations of people, clattering of vessels, children playing, horns and sounds of different vehicles. There can be the sound of something falling, the sound of somebody's footsteps, the sound of television, music system or radio, the sound of birds, the sound of dogs barking or fighting. There can also be the sound of water flowing or a whistle blowing or somebody laughing or crying. When there are no sounds, try to perceive the sound of silence. Feel the stillness.
- Try to detect every type of sound around you. If you hear the sound of an aeroplane in the sky, you will find different planes making different sounds. Try to identify even the minutest of sounds. Listen to at least five different sounds — loud, medium or subtle.
- After having listened to different sounds, ask yourself, 'Am I these sounds?' The reply will come from within you, 'I am not these sounds; I am the one who is identifying these sounds.' Then turn around and see who this hearer is, that is, who is the ear of the ear. Tell yourself, 'I am not the sound.'
- Concentrate on the atmosphere and feel whether it is hot or cold or dry or humid; whether the body feels light or heavy; whether there is a swift breeze or a gentle wind or fresh air or less air.
- If you are able to feel the air, the heat or cold, ask yourself, 'Am I this atmosphere?' A reply will emerge, 'No, I am not this atmosphere. I am the one who is perceiving this atmosphere.' Then tell yourself, 'Turn around' and find the one who is knowing. Tell yourself, 'I am not this atmosphere.'
- Now concentrate your attention on your body. If there is stiffness or pain in any part of the body, just check it with experience. Do not let the body move even a bit.

- In the whole body, where lightness or heaviness is felt, where clothes are tight, or where the air touches, where itching or dryness is felt, where there is sweating, where there is a burning sensation — feel those parts. This way identify and see all the subtle or gross sensations inside and outside the body.
- Here 'seeing' means 'knowing'. Do not imagine anything; just feel what's happening in or on the body. Do not drive away the feeling of what is happening at present. Do not consider that as feeling good or bad; just feel it as it is. After seeing all the sensations, after knowing what is happening in the whole body, ask yourself, 'Am I these sensations?' The reply will be, 'No, I am not these sensations; I am the knower of these.' Then immediately turn around and shift to the knower, reaching inside. Tell yourself, 'I am not these sensations.'
- Focus your attention on your breathing. Just watch how the breathing takes place. Observe through which nostril you inhale and through which nostril you exhale. When the breath enters inside, feel it going in. When the breath is exhaled, feel it coming out.
- When the breath goes through your nose and dashes against the opening of the nostril, you should feel the dashing of the breath. Feel deeply whether the air that is inhaled or exhaled is warm or cold.
- If your attention goes astray in between, bring it back on breathing again. Whether the breath enters silently or by making a sound, whether it comes out silently or with a sound — perceive this too. Whether the breath is shallow, deep or heavy, keep feeling it without labelling it.
- Whether the breath emerges through the left nostril or the right, continue to observe it. In this way, you prepare for meditation and move towards self-meditation (meditation on the self). Ask yourself, 'Am I this breath?' The reply will emerge, 'No, I am not this breath. I am the knower of the

breath.' Now know this knower and tell yourself, 'I am not the breath.'

- Shift your attention from breathing to focus it on the thoughts that arise within. Watch the thought that arises in your mind and after looking at it, watch the next thought that arises. There is no need to pursue any thought. Just watch a thought and say, 'Next.' If you get a thought such as, 'No thought is coming at all', then understand that this too is a thought. After seeing it, say, 'Next.' As you go on watching thoughts, you will also feel the joy of detachment from thoughts. Watch all the thoughts that arise in the mind and ask yourself, 'Am I these thoughts?' The reply will come, 'No, I am not thoughts; I am the knower of thoughts.' Now know that knower. Without moving the body, know the thoughts, and tell yourself, 'I am not these thoughts.'
- Shift your focus to your hands. Observe the feelings in the hands. Take your attention to your arms and experience how you feel there. See whether you are able to feel the arms or not or whether they feel heavy or light. Just know whatever you feel. Ask yourself, 'Am I these hands?' The reply will appear, 'No, I am not these hands, I am the knower of these hands.' Immediately turn your attention back within and know the one who is knowing these hands. Even if you are unable to know the knower (your true self), continue the meditation without getting disappointed.
- Now take your attention to your legs. If you are not the hands, then who are you? To know this, divert your attention to your legs. See whether you are able to feel your legs or not, whether there is pressure on them or lightness in them. Without putting a label of good or bad, ask yourself, 'Am I these legs?' The reply will come, 'No, I am the knower of these legs.' Then know that knower and tell yourself, 'I am not the legs.' If you are not the legs, then who are you? Ask yourself this question.

- To find the answer, take your attention to the back. See how your back feels. Just know how it feels from the shoulders to the waist — whether it feels light, heavy, painful or if there is any pressure. Ask yourself, 'Am I this back?' The reply will come, 'No, I am the knower of this back.' Shifting your focus within, know that knower and tell yourself, 'I am not this back.'
- Now bring your attention to your torso and the heart. Continue to know how the whole region feels. Ask yourself, 'Am I the stomach, am I the heart, am I the neck, am I the shoulders? If I am not all these, then who am I? I am the knower of all these.' Immediately shift your attention and know that knower.
- Now focus your attention on your face. If you are not the torso, then feel your face. See whether you are able to feel your face or not, whether you feel lightness on the face or some sweat on it. Check if you feel pressure on the eyes or do the eyes feel light. Then ask yourself, 'Am I this face?' The reply will come, 'No, I am the knower of this face.' Shift your focus and know that knower.
- Tell yourself, 'I am not this face, I am not this body, I am not the parts of this body, I am not the breath that is going on in the body, I am not the thoughts, I am not the mind which is nothing but a bundle of thoughts; then who am I? I am the knower of these. I am associated with this body to meditate on the self and to know the self.' As soon as you get this understanding, your attachment to the body will break. You will use your body, not vice versa. Continuing to remain in this state of realisation, open your eyes after some time.
- While being in the same experience, go outside for a walk. Watch your body walk.

Contemplate on the understanding that you received, the freshness and the internal energy you attained and the shifting you got from this experience. Contemplate also on what you learnt and understood from complete meditation. This understanding, the awareness, will transform you and stabilise you on self-realisation.

In the state of *samadhi*, the viewer becomes the seen, i.e. the one who sees, becomes the seen for himself. The one who sees and the seen become one.

Chapter Eight

Arrows of Delusion and the Shield of Awareness

Maintain Awareness, Become Capable

Man lives in a world of illusion (*maya*) and is prey to illusions (greed, fear, lust, attachment, hatred, etc.). After learning the secrets of life, man learns the technique of evading illusion. You can understand this from the following story and then contemplate over it.

There is a village where dangers perpetually lay in wait to strike. Anyone visiting this village became vulnerable to its assault. It could not be determined from which direction he would be attacked. It could be a spear that could pierce his body, or stones that hit him or dust flung into his eyes. As he did not know from where and when he could be attacked, he therefore could not dodge the attack. Now if you were to be asked to visit such a village for an important assignment, how would you go there?

Since you *have to* accomplish the task, you get ready to visit that village. At the entrance to the village, you find someone seated to interview you to gauge your ability to survive in the village. You will wonder, 'What is so special about this village? I have been to so many other villages before; I will definitely accomplish my job in this village and return with success.' However, the person who interviews you knows the village and wants to ascertain if you are capable of returning unscathed. He notices that on arrival you look well dressed, in good health and beaming with a smile on your face; but he wonders what your condition would be on your return from the village! He explains the need for this interview to you.

The congregation of truth-seekers

The congregation of truth-seekers (*satsang*) and truth discourses are essentially a part of such an interview. When people attend truth discourses, in reality they are being interviewed — 'After the discourse when you go back to the illusory world, what would be your state when you return to the truth-congregation next time?' The faces of people attending the congregation bear testimony to who would return unscathed. The smiling faces indicate that these faces belong to those who worked properly on the teachings and succeeded in evading the assaults of the illusory world. Likewise, disturbed faces indicate that they had not worked on the teachings and were subject to assaults.

When we live in the world of illusion, we return wounded. Although we may be unharmed in the physical sense, we are wounded at heart. We return with wounds, false beliefs and notions within. In that sense, we are deeply wounded. If we harbour hatred or envy towards people, it implies that we return in a wounded state.

Nurture your awareness

In this illusory world, you ought to first build awareness — the arrow which is short at you will create a certain sound; are you able to hear that sound? If you are not alert, you will not be able to catch that sound. If you miss the sound, the arrow will pierce you. It will then be too late. You should realise beforehand, 'if only I could be more alert, I would be able to escape the attack.'

In this example, the arrows represent the censure, criticism and abuse thrown at you. If someone swears at you, you reciprocate and snap back at him tenfold. It is later that you realise you should have been more alert; it is too late if the arrow (of abuse) has already pierced you, thereby wounding you. Therefore, you ought to train your attention (awareness).

It is observed where your attention is

For this reason, it is essential that every person reaching the village is interviewed before he enters the world. During the interview, his awareness and attention are examined by being asked certain questions and intermittently the interviewer snaps his fingers. When the person's attention is drawn towards the fingers or the snapping sound, he is smacked on the head with the other hand to check if he has been able to discern who has smacked him.

This is observed in the context of children too. If you hit a child on his head and stand back quietly, feigning ignorance, the child starts looking around, wondering who has hit him. This is because the qualities of attention and awareness have not received adequate training in children. They are in the preparatory stage during the early years.

Attention is trained in truth congregation

Similarly, in a congregation of truth-seekers, the seekers are hit on the head (figuratively speaking) to check if they noticed it. Otherwise, the person who is hit may live under the false impression that someone else has been smacked. For instance, when a person hears a loud thud from a room, he rushes into the room to ask the person sitting in the room, "What happened? Did something fall?" The other person replies, "My shirt fell down." The first person exclaims, "The shirt fell? But how come there was such a loud thud?" The other person replies, "Because I was inside the shirt."

From this example it becomes evident that you need to keep your attention under observation even while working. There needs to be some system to help you focus attention on your attention. The congregation of truth-seekers is meant to achieve this purpose.

With awareness, attention is focused on itself

From the interview it can be ascertained whether a person is fit to enter the village (world) or not. If the person is not trained to be aware and to focus on the right place at the right time, he is advised to refrain from entering the village for his own well-being. If the person understands and has trust, he will say, "If this is a village where one can be assaulted from any quarter in any manner, I will come here only after prior preparation." It is commonsense to gain information about a new place that you are about to visit. People gather information about avenues for food and entertainment about the place they plan to visit, but they do not bother to learn where they must focus their attention on reaching that place. When some people plan to travel abroad, they often wonder, 'When abroad, where should we focus our attention?' They are then advised, "Ask yourself, every now and then, whether by changing your place, does your inner experience of being change?" If you remember this, your attention will remain focused on itself.

Never give in to excuses offered by the mind. Those who concede to excuses of their minds never achieve their objective in life. They perish without realising the invaluable secrets of life.

Chapter Nine

Train Your Attention

Awaken Your Understanding

What is the purpose of meditation? When people do notknow the purpose, they practise some techniques of concentration, wrongly assuming it to be meditation. They do not know the real meaning of meditation. When and where should man's attention be focused?

Man's attention should be trained to such an extent that it automatically focuses where needed, depending on the context and condition. Why is it essential to focus our attention? We have never been taught this. If we observe people, we will notice where their eyes drift. A person walks down the street, but do his eyes rove? The television is switched on and the channels are switched on, but where do the ears of the viewer stray? The delectable aroma of food whiffs around, but where does the sense of smell disappear? There is need for comfort and tenderness, but where has the sense of touch gone? This means that man is present at one place whilst his attention stays elsewhere.

Where does the mind get entangled?

When attention wishes to re-establish itself, it pays attention to where the attention is focused. We should be aware of where our attention is. While walking down the street, try this exercise: Ask yourself, 'Where's your attention?' This will help you identify where your attention wanders without your notice. Your attention gets entangled in some issues, stuck in some others and slips away from many to get engrossed in certain other matters. For example our attention gets stuck on a film poster or is lost in a picturesque landscape or slips away from the garbage stench or rests on delicious sweets. This requires you to pay attention to where your attention wanders off. Having known this, you will be able to attend to your attention properly.

False notions since childhood

If you divert your attention even a little, you will see some new aspects emerging that you had never witnessed before as you have never been given to understand what meditation is and what it is not. No one had told you, 'Turn inward; where is your attention?'

Your attention has already been trained on some aspects. Ever since childhood, your attention was trained by people whose attention was on the wrong things (*atej dhyani*). As these people did not know where they were expected to focus their attention, they imparted the same faulty training to their children. For example, watching their parents make remarks over food, children too begin to do the same on growing up, or on seeing their parents mock others' attire, children tend to do the same. They also learn to repeat the same words as their parents do.

Children unknowingly make use of the same vocabulary as their parents. On growing up, they do not reflect on where they picked up the words that emerge from their mouths. No one pays attention to this aspect. When a child chooses clothes for himself, why is he liable to choose those very clothes? No one reflects on this. The child also declares, "I chose this dress", although it is not he who knows how to choose. The fact is that you choose whatever others tend to choose. If today you buy a costume, which goes out of trend tomorrow, then you prefer not to wear it again. But you do not reflect on the fact that you are not dressing according to your judgement.

However, when you begin to hear statements like, 'Awaken your understanding,' you start becoming aware. If people stop exercising their bodies, would you stop too? If at that time you say, 'Regardless of whether people workout or not, I am convinced that exercise is essential for my fitness; therefore I will exercise,' it would mean that your understanding has matured; your power of discrimination has awakened.

If meditation does not awaken your power of discrimination, it actually is an obstacle. With the power of discrimination, the obstacle can be converted into a cause for true meditation.

Chapter Ten

Shifting from Attention Towards Meditation on the Self

Awaken the Power of Discrimination and Self-respect

If the power of discrimination does not get awakened through meditation, then such meditation becomes anti-meditation, proving an obstacle in spiritual progress. Whatever so-called meditations people engage in today, it amounts to anti-meditation in reality. When the true meaning of meditation is lost, a need for a new terminology for meditation is felt. What is believed to be meditation, in reality is anti-meditation, an impediment to true progress! Very few people meditate in the true sense. Most people practise anti-meditation, which can never lead anyone to the true purpose of meditation. Once you get stuck in anti-meditation, mystical powers or short-term benefits of meditation, it no longer remains true meditation.

Benefits of meditation

People indulge in various strange activities in the name of meditation by resorting to jumping, spiritual entertainment or some such activities. What was attention meant to be? Where was it that our attention should have been focused? What is the first thing that attention should have been given? Once you understand these various aspects, you will be able to appreciate what can be achieved through meditation. If you pay attention to your attention, if you frequently remember to turn inward and check where your attention is, you can benefit immensely from meditation.

Meditation raises your sensitivity

From the same example of the village, we could gather that the people who entered the village were in good health. On attending the congregation of truth-seekers (*satsang*), they appeared wounded. Their eyes smarted with dust. However, self-respect awakens with the feeling, 'I don't want to get wounded again.' The Buddha's self-respect was also aroused in the same way when he contemplated, 'When I'll grow old, I will be like this old person. Yashodhara (wife) too will grow old and so will my father!' He was wounded and shaken by these facts and his self-respect was aroused. On getting wounded, you ought to be sensitive to that wound. Meditation makes you sensitive; otherwise you continue to suffer, as you lack sensitivity. The hatred you have for others troubles you, yet you allow it to continue. You harbour feelings of hatred for a long period of time. The person whose self-respect is awakened cannot tolerate such suffering for long. He will tell himself, 'If my feeling of hatred towards someone is causing me distress, I need to get rid of it.' This way, self-respect is awakened within very few people.

Congregation of truth-seekers — a conducive environment for acquiring knowledge

One who is awakened begins to seek the path of liberation from miseries. Wandering in search of the path, he reaches a congregation of truth-seekers (*satsang*), where he learns as to when and from where he is attacked. To learn this, there is a technique, an understanding, an instrument, a shield. Once you obtain it, you will learn to be alert and thus protect yourself. If such knowledge does exist, you ought to learn it. Those, whose self-respect is awakened, join the congregation and learn about it. They are interviewed and tested by receiving a smack (figuratively speaking) on the head. This testing is good since it is to their advantage and is conducted in a conducive environment. It is not meant to trouble them or make them suffer. In fact, testing helps to train them, so that when they return to the world, they can shield themselves against wounds.

Instead of learning how to avoid getting hurt, you learn: 'How bad the world is! The world will never improve; it will remain the same. It is not worth living in this world; however, as we should not put an end to our life, we have to go on.' People live with such false notions. Just see what you were supposed to learn from the world and what you end up learning! If a scientist were to draw such conclusions, there would have never been any discovery or invention. The instruments, that could be used for the convenience and security of mankind and which could have led to the highest expression of the self, start causing trouble. A scientist realises that whatever experiment is carried out should lead him to the right conclusion. The right outcome should be drawn from it. If you get stuck in false assumptions, you tend to hand over the same false beliefs and notions to future generations.

Awaken self-respect

Some, whose self-respect is awakened, no longer suffer the same humiliations from the world as they suffered earlier. How much suffering did Jesus have to go through — he was crucified, his body was tortured. But, internally, he had the understanding of the ultimate truth and was enjoying the highest expression of the self. As he had stopped getting affected from within, he felt mercy and love for his torturers even at the time of his crucifixion. No wounds or trials and tribulations from the external world could disturb him.

In meditation, poison becomes nectar

Socrates was given poison, but he converted the poison into an instrument of contemplation. As the poison started acting on his body, his legs stopped functioning; gradually paralysis sets in to move towards his heart and brain. Yet, he calmly continued to narrate his condition. From this instance we can gather that true meditation was in action.

Socrates was able to witness his body die and perceived it as an amazing experience. He was eager to experience it at the earliest. He could not have resisted the effect of poison as deluded people of the world had inflicted such a punishment on him. Therefore, he accepted their verdict in such a manner that the poison became an object of meditation. The poison could not hurt Socrates from within. His body lay dying, but it could not bring about any change in his inner state of being. He remained the same within.

Stop getting affected from within

Jesus was inflicted a lot of physical wounds, but none could injure him from within. His inner state remained unaffected. The one whose attention is trained, whose attention can return to attention (self), that is the one who is able to meditate on the self, cannot get injured by wounds inflicted by the external world. As the external wounds are apparent, you tend to get swayed by them and try to safeguard yourself from them. You do not pay attention to those injuries, which are invisible from the outside but lie hidden within. Externally a person may appear well educated and mature, but within he may be seething with anger and burning with vengeance and filled with ego. As a result he is unable to enjoy the happiness that life has to offer. He is afraid of being killed or losing his position and status. He is not able to understand pain. He does not seek any treatment for this illness as nobody is there to guide him and neither does he see anyone getting treated or cured for this ailment. He finds people madly pursuing power and status; thus he too turns to participate in this blind race. Not for a moment does he stop to think that all this should stop.

Meditation makes you sensitive. Otherwise man becomes insensitive towards his tendencies, patterns and troubles.

Chapter Eleven

Purify Your Mind

The *Mantra* for Meditation

When will this blind race end? When we see someone contemplating or meditating, or when we, through contemplation, witness the invisible truth, this blind race will come to an end. Till now we may have been waiting for others to start meditating, so that we could follow them. With such an approach, we commit a huge blunder. Regardless of whether others meditate or not, we ought to begin because by now we have realised the benefits of meditation which are not apparent. The visible, tangible benefits are merely a bonus.

We can see the benefits of bathing and this prompts us to bathe daily. However, we cannot see the benefits of bathing (purifying) our mind because this purification is at a subtler level and invisible at the gross level. These inner changes cannot be seen from outside. We are used to doing things to receive appreciation and admiration from others. When we take a bath, we expect people to compliment us, "You look so fresh!" However, when we cleanse ourselves from within, no one compliments us by saying, "You are revelling in bright love (*tej prem*), bright happiness (*tej anand*)." Thus you do not want to meditate. You wait for others to begin first. You continue to do what people tell you to do. This is not the right kind of understanding.

Begin with right understanding

Your understanding tells you to start working on the right things, regardless of whether others perceive them to be right or not. You need to work towards your final goal which is the sole purpose of human life. No matter whether others tread this path or not, you ought to begin on the path of truth.

If there is sorrow, then there is also a way to find liberation from sorrow. If there is a wound, then there is also a way to cure it. Start seeking the solution.

Despite not knowing the solution, great saints like the Buddha relinquished the blind race (for acquisition of power, wealth and status) to pursue the truth. After performing meditation, they reached a state where complete wisdom awakened. For you, the truth congregation is already available, the final discourses are ready, and all the facilities are in place; all you need to do is to avail of it by making a beginning. You need to be alert before being hit and hurt by the illusory world.

Always remember the meditation *mantra*

Where exactly do all the senses related to the eyes, ears, skin, nose and tongue keep wandering, where do they get entangled, where do they slip from and why? Where should you get attached and where should you be detached? Where should you start focusing and wherefrom should you remove your focus? With what should you unite and what should you get separated from? When you clearly understand this, things begin to happen accordingly. You will be immediately reminded, 'Turn inward; where is your attention? What are you involved in? This is not what you wanted. You never wanted to be entangled here; then how did you get trapped here?' Initially you may find it arduous to pull your attention away from the sense objects. The mind finds it difficult to move away from attractions, such as delicious food, beautiful scenery and melodious music. A cricket match is being broadcast and is nearing its final result, but someone tells you, "Let's go out." You will then be reminded to turn inwards; where is your attention? Such occasions are opportunities to focus your attention at the right place. However, you lose that opportunity. You can easily find out later who won the match and who lost. Therefore, there is no need to be so engrossed in any game.

Through experiments, man learns more about himself

Those who experiment with truth are able to come out of the delusions of this illusory world. Those who do not experiment are never able to emerge from it. A person says, 'I never go out alone. I need the company of friends to watch a movie. I always need someone to accompany me.' He is asked to try and go out alone to watch a film. People are not ready to experiment. Those who have carried out this experiment have realised the dialogue that goes on within the mind. What does the mind say during the intermission of the movie? When you see strangers all around, how do you feel? It is only when man goes through this experience that he is able to learn about himself.

Whenever you get the opportunity to train your attention, exercise your resolve and willpower. You are made to prepare yourself before meditation. You are made aware of where the focus of your attention is; your self-respect is awakened and you are clearly explained what is the purpose of all this. Soon you will be convinced of the need to pay attention to your attention. If you do not focus on your attention, you will be lost in a maze of delusions. If at least ten persons were to remind you daily that you are wounded, you may think of getting out of it. Since nobody is telling you, your self-respect does not awaken. You try to cover up your wounds; you hide them. As long as you are able to hide them, you continue to live without treating them. If you want to get them treated, do not hide them.

How is your attention? It wanders here and there when you walk down the street; it wanders when you are at home; it wanders when you are alone; it wanders when you are in the midst of people. Thus your attention is always wandering. Such is the nature of your attention. Do not feel bad if your attention is not trained. Instead, it means that you have come to know your ailment. Therefore, the Buddha proclaimed the first noble (fundamental) truth: 'Observe sorrow and you will transcend it. If you are reluctant to observe it, you will never come out of it. Become sensitive.' When you observe the suffering you are going through at this moment in its entirety, you will end up saying, 'Now this is enough. I am not going to live like this any more. I would like to transcend this.' In this manner your self-respect will awaken.

So far you have understood the necessity of awareness and attention (focus), the kind of interview the congregation of truth-seekers need and the type of knocks you get on the head. One who is sensitive understands what is being said and thinks: '*Turn inward, where is your attention?* It was indeed meant for me. Indeed, it is my focus that always keeps on wandering.' One who is insensitive will think, 'This was meant for someone else. That other fellow commits such mistakes. I never get entangled. I am so balanced. Therefore, this is not meant for me.'

Everyone ought to pay attention to where his or her attention is directed. It does not suffice to merely check where the attention is focused externally. You ought to be sure of where your attention should be and where it should turn back. If you are sure of this, then the statement, 'Turn inward; where is your attention?' will act like a *mantra* for you.

During the course of the day, often tell yourself, 'Turn inward; where is your attention?' Thus you will be reminded, 'My attention is on so-and-so object, but where is it supposed to be?' The answer will come from within, directing you to be in the present or at the heart. This way you will immediately return to your heart. When feasible, close your eyes and withdraw your attention to your heart. Where it is not possible, focus your attention on your heart, keeping your eyes open. 'The experiencer experiences the experiencer (self) in the experience.' If you can experience this, then you will be able to really feel it. You will then realise that the one who sees, that what is seen and the experience of seeing are all one and the same. The artist, the artifact and art are one and the same. If all merge into one, then only the art, the experience of seeing, remains. Then the viewer and the seen dissolve, as it were. This is the peak. After understanding this, think how you can train your attention to attain this peak, the final goal. If you understand its need, you will start working on it. It is for this reason that its importance was explained at the outset, so that you could focus your attention in the right direction.

Be consistent in meditation

Consistency is the key to success. Those who commence with meditation and pursue it with consistency realise this secret. Many people say, "We have been meditating daily for so many years. And for a long time, there were no discernible benefits from it."

Whoever takes to meditation is warned that contrary thoughts like these would plague the mind frequently. Such a mind will attempt to dissuade you by raising questions like, 'You have been in meditation for so long. What have you achieved?' Even if you do not see any benefit, you ought to continue with meditation. Those who follow this instruction are sure to succeed. You should practise meditation as long as possible without bothering about the results. You should certainly check whether you are meditating properly or not, but do not check whether it is paying off or not; never check the experience. Let this go on without a break.

Those, who started with meditation and persisted with the practice consistently, realised that consistency is the key to success.

Chapter Twelve

What is not Meditation?

True Meditation

Attention is not meditation

What is not meditation? Who you are not? You are that which remains after these two questions are answered. What you are not? When you ask this question, you realise that you are neither this nor that. Finally, after negating everything conceivable, whatever remains is what you are. In the same way, let us understand what is not meditation. Very often, people mistake meditation to mean attention. In the Hindi language, the same word *'dhyan'* is used for both meditation and attention. Likewise, the English language permits the use of the word 'meditation' to mean reflection or contemplation. True meditation is neither contemplation nor attention; it refers to meditation on the true self. Hence a new word has been given to meditation which is 'self-meditation'.

Concentration is not meditation

Some people mistake concentration for meditation. Focusing the mind on a particular object is concentration but concentration is not meditation; rather, it is the beginning of meditation. To concentrate and then remain focused on a given subject is the beginning of meditation. The convergence of all thoughts on a single point marks preparation for meditation. If you are not able to concentrate fully, you cannot understand the subject thoroughly. When children study, they often need to read the same lesson repeatedly as their concentration is weak. If our concentration is weak and we have to read the same topic innumerable times, we realise how important concentration is. The ability to concentrate is good; but it does not imply meditation. Concentration is essential as it is the stepping-stone to meditation. However, the stepping-stone is not the goal.

Mystical powers have nothing to do with true meditation

One can attain mystical powers (*siddhi*) through the practice of concentration. However, those who have attained such mystical powers have wrongly associated such powers with spirituality. For instance, the practice of awakening the power of *kundalini* is wrongly believed to be spiritual. (*Kundalini* is considered to be a system of *chakras* [vortices] or energy-regulating centres located approximately along the spinal axis of the body). As people are unaware of what is the actual meaning of the power of *kundalini* and what are the *chakras*, they associate them with spirituality without being sceptical about it. Spirituality has nothing to do with these things. When you begin to know your true self, when you meditate on the self, when you shift to (identify with) your true nature which is formless, then true meditation takes place. Do not mistake concentration for meditation. Concentration can help attain mystical powers but not everyone can possess mystical powers which are considered miraculous. Thus people are led to believe that these powers are spiritual. Some people who wander as celibates, clad in saffron robes, are wrongly considered spiritual. Some of them take to meditation with the desire to acquire mystical powers by repeatedly uttering *mantras* (performing *jap*). The occult powers gained through repeated utterances of *mantras* only inflate their ego, imparting a false sense of happiness, which in turn leads to further delusions on being stuck in these practices.

The ego (individuality) desires that we put on wondrous acts and show off to the world. Those who fail to prove themselves in their studies or other fields get attracted to occult practices. When they fail to achieve anything in the external world, they put on the garb of celibacy and flaunt mystical powers to cover up for the resentment built inside due to their failures. They think, 'No one has ever given me any attention. Now, I will do something that will make people look up to me.' Those who are not given enough attention during their childhood develop such a kind of deep-rooted desire during their early years. After growing up, they invariably attempt to do something that will draw the attention of the people. They ignore what wisdom tells them. They ruin their lives in the process. Those who crave for attention end up spending their lives putting on a false façade. Whatever they do is with the intent of putting on a show for people. By doing so, they want to convey, 'See, what I am capable of! You assumed I was good-for-nothing. Look at what I have achieved! Can you achieve such power?'

Ninety-nine per cent of such people are caught in the pursuit of mystical powers due to their deep-rooted craving for recognition. In reality they tend to suffer from deep misery after attaining these powers. They do not disclose the turmoil that they experience within. How can they admit their distress and suffering that they are going through due to attainment of such powers? How can they reveal their dependence on relaxants or anti-depressants to get sleep? These powers trouble them a lot from within, leading to terrible agony. They long for peace and relaxation in their lives. This happens because they have not attained these powers under right guidance.

Some mystics have confessed their condition out of honesty or for monetary gains from journalists. This revealed their true condition, deluded as they were in their pursuit of mystical powers. They do get recognition from people but actually they are troubled within as they have never practised true meditation. They have never attempted to find out who they were in essence. Being fascinated by their mystical powers, they received respect, got free meals, had their feet touched by their followers who surrounded them to seek their blessings.

Being highly respected by people, they ended up being recognised as spiritual masters. People do not realise that these so-called mystics have nothing to do with spirituality. When their income from their followers came to an end, they found themselves in a pitiable condition and revealed their plight to journalists. They no longer advised people to pursue mystical powers. When these facts came out, it made people aware about the gross misunderstanding regarding meditation: about how people in the name of meditation have strayed away. Therefore, never get entangled in the pursuit of mystical powers.

Let concentration culminate in meditation on the self

The practice of concentration leads to the attainment of mystical powers because the human body is verily a wonder of wonders. If one were to dedicate his entire life towards awakening the hidden powers of the body-mind mechanism, that would not suffice. Therefore, one should not get into this pursuit in the first place. We can derive the benefit of concentration for moving towards self-meditation, rather than using it in the pursuit of such powers. If one comes to know about any event before it occurs, one feels pleased and pronounces to the world, "I knew that this event was going to occur well in advance; I told you so!" The feeling of 'I knew what others did not' inflates the ego of the individual, prompting blind believers to flock around him to find out if they would accomplish a given task or not. If the task does get accomplished, then the individual feels no qualms in saying, "Look, I had told you. My forecast can never go wrong. I had told you that such and such event will occur by reading the lines on your palm." This way such people keep fostering their own egos. They are stuck in anti-meditation. Their concentration becomes anti-meditation.

Contemplation is not meditation

Contemplation is not meditation. If someone believes that he is meditating by reflecting on a particular subject, he is mistaken. Contemplation only acts like a bridge that leads us to the silence within. There are numerous topics that one can contemplate on; therefore, the purer the contemplation is, the more effective it will be. How does one choose the topic for contemplation? Those who worship through contemplation (*manan upasana*) realise how they can improve their shortcomings and overcome them through meticulous contemplation. It also raises their understanding and speeds up their growth towards realising the inner silence. There are many techniques for concentrating the mind; there are many topics for contemplation; however, if we contemplate on the right topic, it can lead us to the state of timeless bliss of being (*samadhi*).

If you want a supporting principle, an aid or a bridge, then let the bridge be such that it leads you to well-being and happiness while purifying the mind. Contemplation is only the means and not the end. Those saints who work like a bridge between man and God have also been called *Tirthankars*. Only the bridge that is instrumental in leading man to attain Godhood is useful. Contemplation is not meditation because true meditation is not the path; it is the destination. If you have grasped the essence of true meditation, you will know it is the destination. People make use of meditation as the means; in that sense, meditation is both the means and the end. In other words, whatever has been commonly understood to be meditation till date is only the path, and true meditation on the self (self-meditation) is the goal.

Concentration is the focus of the mind on one topic to the exclusion of all other topics. Concentration is not meditation; rather, it is the preparatory step towards meditation.

Chapter Thirteen

Meditation is Your True Nature

Know Your Attribute

So far you have understood what meditation is not. Meditation is not something distinct or apart from what needs to be gained and acted upon. The truth is that *you are meditation*. Let us understand this in depth. When we realise the true import of the statement, 'You are meditation,' we find that though the statement seems illogical, nonetheless it is the truth. We are not separate from meditation. We are meditation. When people ask questions such as, "How to meditate?", "How to get into the state of meditation?", they are told, "You need not meditate. You need to understand that you are meditation in essence." Many people are not convinced by such an answer, as they cannot conceive as to how they themselves can be meditation. They are then told that meditation is their religion.

Meditation is our religion, i.e. our essential nature. Just as the nature of water is wet, in the same way, meditation is the fundamental nature or attribute of our true being. We ought to be established in our true nature, implying that we should be stabilised in meditation. In this state, we can clearly see who we are and how the body is serving as an instrument to help me experience my true self. It is because of the presence of this body that I can experience my *being*. The body is just kept beside you. Till today, you lived with the notion that you are within your body. However, the body is actually meant to be a mirror kept beside you. It enables you to experience yourself, just as a fan kept beside you enables you to experience the breeze as well as your own body (that senses the breeze). If the fan is taken away, you will not be able to experience your body (in the absence of the sensation of breeze). Similarly, you can assume that the body (like the fan) has been kept near you so that you can experience yourself (your true self). This experience is not a mere physical experience of the senses; rather, it is the awareness of your existence or your original state of being.

There will be detachment towards the body

If your body were to be taken away from you for some time, you would say, "I am not able to experience myself. The experience of my being has stopped." And when the body is again kept near you, you again begin to experience yourself. In this way, gradually you will realise that you are not the body and feel detachment towards it. You will then say, 'It does not matter whether the body is present or not; whether the body is fair or dark complexioned; whether it is tall or short; all this simply makes no difference.' If you were given a body and told that it will remain with you for eighty years, you will say, 'Alright, any body will do'. If you were then told that this body would expire after eighty years, you would say, 'Fine. What's the big deal!' As long as the body is available, you will make use of it. When it is not there, you would still be fine as you will still exist. You were always there and you will always be; you are eternal. When you are convinced about this, you will realise that this is merely your gross (physical) body. After the gross body is cast away, the subtle body will be at your service. As long as the gross body is available, make use of it to express your qualities.

In this way, realise that the body is just kept with you, and by its presence you are able to experience your true being. You will then give a pat on the back (of your body) intermittently and tell your body, 'You are doing a good job. Stay beside me, so that I can express my nature.' When we are able to clearly see this, the mechanism that was programmed in the body due to which it kept on thinking something on its own, will come to an end. Let us understand this with the help of an example. An individual seated beside you constantly keeps muttering to himself, "This person did this... That person did that... He should not have done this... She should not have done that... When will I finish with my studies?... When will this happen?... When will that be completed?..." You will feel a bit disturbed and wonder, 'Why is this person grumbling? He is not allowing me to meditate; I am unable to experience the self.' You will then try to find the cause of his grumbling as well as whose fault it is — his or yours? That is when you realise that whenever you move away from (forget) your true nature, he starts muttering. When you are established in your true nature, his muttering ceases. (This man symbolises your body-mind and 'you' represent your true self). He then verbalises only the thoughts arising from your true self. Then any words expressed through that body will be a discourse. The great saint Tukaram told people, "I am not reciting any *Upanishad* (religious text). If the words that are being expressed through my body, akin to the words arising from God, happen to match the contents in the *Upanishad*, what can I do?"

The experience is within all of us

It is not necessary to be educated or well-read to experience the self. This experience is within all of us. Even if it is an illiterate person, the experience is within him as well. Self-realisation is not restricted to urban residents or the princes of aristocratic families. A simple villager had self-expression nothing short of the highest *Upanishads*. People were astounded and wondered how such words of wisdom could emanate from this illiterate man. This happened because it became clear to those who attained self-realisation that the body was just kept nearby and the experience of the self was expressing itself. Earlier, when the mind used to grumble, we felt that there was something wrong with the mind or it was due to past deeds. We failed to recognise mistakes made in the present.

Become established in your true nature

As we do not meditate on the self, we have deviated from our true nature. People consider religion to mean Hinduism, Christianity, Islam, Buddhism, Jainism, etc. The true meaning of religion is to abide by one's true nature.When we move away from our true nature, it means that we become non-religious. If this is the basis of religion, how many such religious people will we find? There would be very few religious people indeed, because the vast majority of people are not established in their true nature, and neither do they want to. To top it all, some people put on a religious garb so that others may consider them religious. People find it easy to accept a person who sets his hair locks in a particular manner, wears particular robes, particular footwear and the rosary, to be religious. However, these have nothing to do with true religion. Being truly religious means returning to one's true nature.

Begin with yourself

Meditation is our religion, our true nature, our attribute. When we are far removed from our true nature, the mind turns to muttering. We need not think, 'What can I do if my body-mind keeps worrying?' We have to take responsibility for this instead of making excuses like, 'No one else is meditating. If others are not doing these things, then why should I?' We ought to understand that it will begin only when we take the initiative. We will have to begin on the basis of understanding and by contemplating, 'Is this essential for me? Has my self-respect awakened? Do I want to continue to be wounded and suffer this way?' The inner wounds are the root wounds. Whatever be our circumstances or state, we should not receive these wounds. When we stop getting wounded, we will be able to say, 'I no longer get wounded as I have now got the shield of meditation. Now I am liberated from all misery.'

The Buddha renounced his kingdom after deep pondering, 'Will I also suffer from old age and sickness one day?' This does not mean that the Buddha did not grow old. His body did become old and sick and perished. Yet, he proclaimed that he had been liberated, implying that he could clearly see his body apart from his self. Earlier, he had the false belief that 'I am the body', which led to misery. When this belief got shattered, he could proclaim himself to be liberated.

Chapter Fourteen

The Triangle of Meditation

Meditation Techniques Involving the Breath, Alphabets and Happy Thoughts

You are given a technique to enter the state of meditation. When you sit for a session of meditation, you begin to work on that technique, but within a few minutes, you forget it. Suddenly you remember it and again start working on the same technique. Continuing the session this way, you finally enter the state of *samadhi*. Since meditation proves helpful to enter into *samadhi*, many techniques have been devised.

The technique of breath

Some people meditate, using the technique of breath. They keep observing the breath as it is inhaled and exhaled, as they have understood the purpose of meditation as '*meditation is the present*'. When we are in the present, we do not need the mind. The mind is needed to run away from the present. To run far away or to escape from the present, the mind is required. Many people meditate by concentrating on inhaling and exhaling. This occurs in the present and not in the past or future. The breath is in the present. When we begin to get stabilised in the present, it is called meditation.

Shift from the technique and go into *samadhi*

You do not feel attached to your breath. Since your breathing is always going on, you do not worry about it. The breath goes in and out of its own accord. You never think that once the breath goes out, it will not return. You do not have any fear about your breath, nor do you feel attachment towards it. You know that it will go on. Hence, focus on the breath is a pure technique. The breath goes in and comes out and you simply observe it doing so.

Later you will learn that there are various techniques to reach the state of *samadhi*. In the state of *samadhi*, the breathing is slow, but one does not realise whether it is going on or not. When such a state is attained, it means you have rightly shifted from the meditation technique to the state of *samadhi*. You began with a technique and then let go of it. You went into a boat, and after crossing the river, you let go of the boat. On letting go of the technique, you enter into *samadhi*. Now you are in the state of *maun* ('bright silence') and *samadhi*.

Samadhi — samay adi (before time)

The word *samadhi* is derived from *samay adi,* meaning 'before time'. *Samadhi* means the state that existed before time. Before the world came into existence, there was no 'time'. 'Time' was perceived only after the world was created. Hence what existed before the creation of the world is called *samadhi* or *samyaant*. When you reach *samyaant*, it is the end of time, and you are then back in *samadhi*. Meditation first begins with a technique. As you begin to grasp the experience of the self, wisdom (the understanding of 'who I am') awakens. The real thing is not understood right at the beginning.

The triad of the Buddha

The Buddha mentioned only three words: good conduct, *samadhi* and wisdom. The Buddha gave this triad to his disciples. Let us understand what this triad is:

- **Good conduct**

  Good conduct means not doing deeds which cause anxiety or disturbance. This includes avoidance of hurting others, stealing, telling lies, eyeing another's wealth or woman. These were some external rules enunciated by the Buddha. The Buddha had also mentioned that one should refrain from killing and violence, because if man were to keep away from violence, his mind would automatically be at peace. Those people are never at peace who indulge in killing and violence.

- ***Samadhi***

  The Buddha said that when man enters *samadhi*, his wisdom awakens. When wisdom awakens, he is able to enter deeper and more often into *samadhi*. In this way the Buddha drew a deep co-relation between *samadhi* and wisdom.

- **Wisdom**

  Wisdom means understanding. When understanding increases, the need for any kind of technique disappears. Man can then enter *samadhi* instantly without the aid of any technique.

Be present in meditation

You do not do anything to fall asleep. You only lie down and sleep catches up. You say, 'God willing, sleep will come.' You do not have to do anything to sleep. Those who *try* to get sleep, are unable to sleep.

When understanding increases, the same happens in meditation too. Without doing anything, by just sitting in the posture of meditation, you can easily reach the state of meditation. To bring about such depth of meditation, the importance of understanding has been stated. If you try to meditate, meditation does not happen. The mind always wants to try. Hence it is given a technique. Meditation is like sleep: if you keep looking for it, you will not get it. If you engage your mind in something else (technique), you will get what you want (*samadhi* or the supreme truth). This is a technique. Hence many techniques have been devised to go into meditation.

If a person remains busy with the technique itself and keeps checking, 'Did anything happen? Did I reach the state of *samadhi*? Did the feeling of the body disappear?', the true purpose of meditation is lost. When you stop worrying about these things and decide to carry on, whether anything happens or not, you are able to enter into meditation faster. Understand this knack, this secret of meditation — that you do not have to do anything in meditation. All you need to do is to be present. The state of a person in meditation is, 'I am present and am receptive to meditation and grace.' After this thought, meditate and do nothing. The emptier your mind becomes the faster you reach the depths of meditation.

Man desires the grace of God in meditation. He has the image of God in his mind. If you are receptive, you can easily sit in the state of *upasana* (just being present). During meditation, you are present in a way that something (the experience of self) comes from God and you are ready to receive it. If you keep checking the grace that is being bestowed on you, then you are not receptive; you are focusing your mind outside. The main purpose of meditation is to enter within.

When you read or listen to the message of truth, you are receptive, and when you speak, you direct your focus outside. In order to receive what comes from God, the lesser the obstacle, the faster you become receptive. The bigger the ego of man, the greater is the obstacle in meditation. The more the ego is surrendered, the more you are able to witness the self (self-realisation). The ego stands in front of the idol of God and asks, 'Where is God? Where is meditation? There is no one in this temple.' One who is wise will say, 'Okay, there is no one. But you move aside. You are the obstacle, you are the obstruction and so you have to move aside.' If we argue with the ego, we will never win. To reduce the stiffness (haughtiness) of the ego, grace is needed. Hence we are advised to just be present during meditation to receive that grace.

The right posture of meditation

Ego or mind is the obstruction between you and meditation. However, if you sit still in meditation despite the ego, grace is bestowed. Bestowal of grace means the self, which is present behind the ego, reduces the stiffness of the ego. Man gets a stiff neck due to the ego and grace is required to undo this stiffness. Grace massages the shoulder of the ego so that its stiffness reduces. After this, the mind is happy and sits quiet. It is then that a glimpse of God (glimpse of self) is obtained. For this glimpse to take place, you just have to be present. Grace comes to you despite the obstacle of the mind because you sit in such a physical and mental posture that you are ready to receive. There is no obstacle to grace from your side. Only your presence is important. In meditation, you are receptive to what is being bestowed on you. When you sit for meditation but forget it in between, then remind yourself, 'I am not sitting here to do anything else. I am seated here to become receptive. My aim is to receive whatever is coming towards me. Hence, I only have to be present.' In such a state, the receiving of grace is the right posture of meditation.

Receptivity increases through idols

In ancient times, in order to increase the receptivity of the meditator, idols of God used to be placed before him. You will now understand the secret behind why idols were invented. On seeing the idol, what do you remember? While meditating, if you open your eyes and your eye falls on the idol, what do you remember? If the meditator has contemplated on the qualities represented in that idol, he will not think of mundane matters; he will remember the only truth.

In order to remind us of all the divine qualities, the qualities are represented symbolically in an idol and many stories are built around it so that on listening to them, we remember all the qualities of God. All the qualities are put into a single idol only to remind you. When man focuses his attention on the idol and contemplates the divine qualities, he becomes receptive for those qualities.

Man, being very weak, is unable to contemplate on the formless God or Universal Self. It is necessary to give him something to turn to. Hence different kinds of idols were created.

The method of alphabets

Some people, when told to contemplate on the qualities of God, fail to remember anything. Such people have been given the method of alphabets. The first letter in the sequence of alphabets is 'A'. 'A' stands for 'Awareness.' Hence one is told to work on increasing awareness and contemplate on the benefits of awareness.

Contemplation on every alphabet in the proper sequence is advised. The letter 'B' stands for 'Buddha'. So contemplate the state of the Buddha. 'B' also stands for '*Bhakti*' (feeling of Divine devotion). Therefore contemplate and meditate on '*Bhakti*'. In this way, you will get trained in contemplation. This is an easy method to contemplate. This will also make you remember the truth even while living in the material world. Otherwise people do remember A, B, C, D... but not the truth. You can now contemplate for hours on every word. Gradually you become habituated to contemplation. A time will come when you will not need the alphabets.

When you use the ABCD method of contemplation, you do not realise when you drift into *samadhi*. As you begin to grasp the self-experience (the experience of your being), you only need to close your eyes and you will reach that state. Initially, the ego used to come in between, but later nothing comes in between. Gradually even without closing your eyes, you will drift into that experience (attention on attention — greatest meditation). When you touch the depths of meditation, you do not need the techniques or rules of meditation you began with.

'Happy thoughts meditation'

Let us learn about the 'happy thoughts meditation'. The prime cause of unhappiness in man are his desires, which arise every moment in his mind. But the desire to be liberated from these desires is a happy thought. In 'happy thoughts meditation', you just have to stroll around and observe what desire arises within you. Watching that desire, tell yourself, 'I am now free of all desires.' You cannot even imagine how wonderful your life would be if you were to get liberated from all desires. There are desires inside you, but you do not know most of them. 'Happy thoughts meditation' helps to bring these desires to light. If desires are not fulfilled, one experiences unhappiness. Meditation saves you from that unhappiness.

During this meditation, you have to be alert to whatever desires arise within you. And tell yourself, 'Now I have no desire. In these ten minutes I will harbour no desires. I am free from desires.' You have to remain desire-free for those ten minutes so that no desire remains within you. You will be able to comprehend some desires as these are the obvious ones. But you will not be able to catch the subtle ones. For example, when watching television, there is an unconscious desire within you which says that no power failure should take place. But you are unable to see this desire. You are able to perceive it only when there is a power failure. You begin to curse the electricity department. From this you realise that you actually desired that there should be no power failure but when hindrances cropped up, unhappiness resulted. But if you have understanding, then even if there is a power failure, you will declare, 'Things are great.'

The time that is allotted to 'happy thoughts meditation' should make you ensure that at least during that period you should remain desire-free. Every person ought to allot some time for 'desire-free meditation'. Do not change your posture during this type of meditation. If sitting, remain seated; if standing, remain standing; if walking, continue walking. A desire will arise in your mind, 'Let me sit for some time or stand for some time,' but you do not have to give in to what the mind says. You should get trained to such an extent in this meditation that you are able to proclaim, 'Even if I am made to sit here for my entire life, it does not matter as I am now desire-free.' When you do this meditation, for the first time you will be able to experience the happiness of freedom. After tasting the freedom from desires, you will progress on the path of meditation.

If your attention is not trained, do not be disappointed by it.
This only means that you have recognised your illness.
After recognising your illness, begin to work on it.
Begin to train your attention.

Chapter Fifteen

The Four Enemies of Meditation

The Obstacles to the Path of Meditation

We have already learnt the prerequisites for meditation. Now let us learn the obstacles that come in the way of meditation. Many obstacles can appear during meditation. Let us understand some of the main ones in brief.

First enemy — disappointment

When man meditates and fails to see any results coming from it, disappointment sets in. A disappointed person is unable to concentrate. He begins to feel drained of all energy. Hence always repeat positive thoughts and just observe the thoughts of disappointment pass by just as dark clouds do. You see clouds from far away and hence you do not get attached to them. Similarly, watch the thoughts of disappointment pass by with a detached feeling. Never say, 'I am disappointed'; say instead, 'Thoughts of disappointment are now passing through my mind.'

Second enemy — doubt

On sitting for meditation, man begins to doubt himself, 'Will I be able to meditate? I don't feel I can meditate. Meditation is for others. What wonderful experiences people share regarding meditation!

I have nothing to share. So I don't think meditation is meant for me.' Self-doubt is one of the most significant enemies that one comes across in meditation. It is among the major enemies of meditation. While meditating, if one does not suffer from self-doubt, then he begins to doubt the guru who has taught him the technique of meditation. Doubts like, 'Why did the master give me this technique? What is his ulterior motive?' begin to appear in man's mind. One side of the mind will want him to stop the meditation as it finds it very boring. Such boredom signifies the death of the mind. It does not want to die and hence asks, 'Why has *this* technique been given? There does not appear to be any benefit from it.'

Thus man begins to doubt even his guru. If he does not doubt himself or his guru, he begins to doubt the meditation technique, the spiritual practice (*sadhana*) imparted to him. 'There are a lot of benefits from this practice. But will I truly attain liberation (*moksha*) through this practice?' When doubts begin to creep in, understand that the enemy has arrived. Recognise this doubt as the enemy and do not commit the foolishness of being taken in by it.

Suppose you read a book entitled *How to Get Rid of Unwanted Guests*. A guest who is staying at your house tells you to avoid reading the book as he finds it useless. Hearing this, will you be taken in by his words? You are reading the book to chase away this very guest, so how can you be taken in by his words? If somebody else were to give you the same advice, then perhaps you may have considered, but in this case, the one to tell you is himself a guest, though he does not think himself to be a guest.

This was only an example to drive home the point that you should not be taken in by what the mind says. When you sit for meditation, the mind may tell you, 'This is wrong… That is not right… You won't be able to meditate. Those who meditated were different kinds of people. With you, so many things have happened. You have such and such a disease. You have pain in your leg… You are not that well-educated, you won't understand it...' When the mind says such things, explain to it, 'It is not necessary to be well educated for meditation. Neither is it necessary that the body should be in perfect condition without any pain. No matter how the body is, meditation can be done with it.' Do not raise any doubts regarding meditation. Chase away this second enemy of meditation at once.

Third enemy — attachment, hatred, thoughts of sensual pleasures

When you sit in meditation, you may recall some adverse events due to which you may begin to get many ideas regarding how you can avenge your opponent. You thereby feel good and satisfied. The ego feels satisfied and says, "This is what I wanted. I always wanted to take my revenge." If thoughts about harming somebody begin to come in your mind, become alert because along with it, cravings, lust and thoughts of sensual pleasure begin to follow. Man has many ambitions. He constantly watches various things due to which many sights enter within him. During meditation, all these scenes begin to emerge like a movie and man gets entangled in it. Later he remembers, 'Oh! I had sat down to meditate and not to do anything else.'

What thoughts begin to arise in your mind when you visit a temple? When you go to a temple, only those thoughts should arise for which you have gone there. If you have to think of other things, then do so after returning home. Beware of this enemy of meditation.

Fourth enemy — laziness or lethargy

The fourth enemy of meditation is laziness or lethargy. After sitting in meditation, if the body does not support you, you begin to doze off. Due to sleep, the mind says, 'Leave meditation alone and go to sleep. In any case, you are not able to do it properly.'

The mind has used its own logic for many years to dupe you. Hence, in meditation too, the mind wants to use its own logic. A spurious coin will not work for long. It works as long as people accept it. When people become aware, the circulation of that coin stops instantly. In the same way, you have to be alert against this fourth enemy of meditation. When the mind says, 'Anyway, nothing is happening through meditation,' tell it, 'It does not matter whether anything happens or not in meditation. If I have to sit for meditation, then I *have to* sit.'

Always remember that for meditation, '*consistency is the key to success.*' Hence do not break the regularity of meditation. If the mind gets too obsessed with thoughts of stopping meditation, then get up and splash some cold water on your face or wipe your face with a wet towel before resuming meditation again. No matter what, decide to make the mind work for the fixed duration of time — this should be your goal.

Such problems appear only in the initial stages of meditation and are termed as 'teething troubles'. When a baby begins to get teeth, it experiences some difficulities but later on, things become easy. Similarly you too will begin to look forward to the arrival of the time for meditation. This is because you begin to derive happiness from meditation.

On reaching the depths of meditation, the mind will no longer find meditation boring. On the contrary, it will feel good and the duration of meditation will increase over time spontaneously. Then, whenever you get a chance, you will slip into meditation. Nobody will even notice that you are meditating; it will become so easy for you.

> ***'You will become what you focus on.'* Making use of this law, you can remain in the state of meditation.**

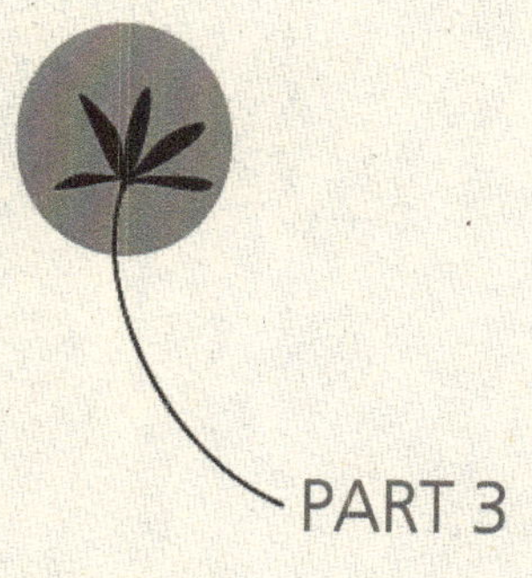

PART 3

Third Supreme Secret of Life

Chapter One

The Secret of Progress

The Wealth of the House of the Supreme

The third supreme secret of life is: *'You gain out of whatever you give. Whatever you take only helps you to sustain.'* The 'gain' in this context pertains to progress. Indeed, it is whatever you give that leads to progress, and whatever you take merely helps you to sustain yourself. Man believes that he will progress when he acquires something, but the secret is, 'Whatever you give becomes the cause of your progress; you gain out of it.'

When you hear these secrets, they sound illogical; they do not appeal to the intellect. However, when reality unfolds, you realise that these secrets are indeed true. In fact, you have already exercised this secret unknowingly. Till today, whatever you had given has led to your progress. This secret also says that you can only give away something that has been kept in your care (by Nature) for someone else. This means that at present you possess it, but it actually belongs to someone else; you just do not know it. When you give a thing to a person, it means actually that thing belongs to him; you have just been a trustee for it for the time being. However, if you give a thing that is your own, the same comes back to you a thousandfold.

The wealth of the 'House of the Supreme'

In the 'House of the Supreme' (on Earth), there is the wealth of love, patience, courage, time, attention and health. Man is endowed with different forms of wealth. If he does not attain these and believes that acquiring money is his only aim, he is bound to repent in the long run. The third secret clearly outlines how money should enter your life. When you put the third secret into practice, you find the money growing in your life and you progress ahead. According to this secret, what is it that you possess and which you can give? If you ponder over this, you will realise that you have the wealth of love, time, physical strength, attention and money. To whatever extent you possess any of these forms of wealth, you can give these to yourself and to others.

From this secret you need to ponder: What is it that has been kept in your care for others? What is it that you have to give? Money represents the wealth that enters your life. Money is a simplified medium for exchange of goods and services. In olden days, people used to follow a barter system, for instance, rice used to be exchanged for wheat. People carried sacks of grain for barter. Today, people carry money. This has made transactions easier. Money was only meant to be an easy and convenient medium for exchange; however, people have forgotten the meaning of money, due to which acquisition and accumulation of money has become the aim of life. Money was supposed to be the means; however, today it has become the end (the goal).

If man does not attain the various forms of wealth, namely courage, love, time, attention and health and believes that acquiring money is his only aim, he is bound to repent in the long run.

Chapter Two

The Asset of Money

A Blessing Should not Become a Curse

Beliefs about money

People carry many false notions and beliefs about money in their mind. Some of these notions are as follows:

- Money is Satan. It is evil.
- Money is God. It is everything.
- Man moves away from spiritualism when money enters his life.
- Money can break friendships (failure to repay a debt can break friendships).
- Money can buy everything.
- By earning more money, one becomes rich.

All these false notions about money should be removed as money cannot buy everything. This is the reason why it is said, '*The person who has only money is very poor.*' Money is not the only wealth in life; there are many other forms of wealth, which are provided by the Almighty to the guests who visit his abode.

Give to yourself as well

You spend money on grocery, laundry, electricity, and other

domestic amenities. Everybody spends money on these necessities, without setting money aside for oneself. The thought of giving money to yourself never occurs to you. You give love to everyone but not to yourself. You spend time with others, but never set aside time for yourself. You pay attention to all others, except yourself. Due to this, the progress that you could have achieved by providing money, love, time and attention to yourself gets stalled.

With the third secret, you need to decide for yourself as to what percentage of your total money you will give yourself. A simple mathematical formula is to divide your total earnings in ten portions, use nine portions for daily expenditure and keep one portion for yourself, regardless of whether you have less or more money. When the false notions about money get shattered, then the poorest too can make ten portions out of his earnings. Else man will continue to believe that when he earns more money, his financial problems would be solved and he would become rich. People who harbour such beliefs are never able to become rich. Instead, they live under constant pressure and always face shortage of money as they have not realised the secret of money.

The seed of prosperity

While working on the third secret of life, you have to abide by the rule that when you have earned 10,000 rupees, you will convince yourself that you have earned only 9,000. The remaining 1,000 rupees will serve as the seed for your prosperity. If you realise this secret, you will be able to turn this seed into a big tree of prosperity. You will be able to rest peacefully under the shade of this tree — enjoy the happiness, and find time to reflect on the truth and put it into practice.

This rule is applicable in all cases, regardless of how much money you have. You may have 10,000 rupees or 100 rupees — it does not matter. Even if you have 100 rupees, you need to divide it into ten portions and keep ten rupees for yourself. Then say to yourself, 'These ten rupees are my asset; these constitute the treasure of my prosperity.' Don't say, 'How can ten rupees be a treasure? How can it be called a treasure?' Even if you feel so, still consider these ten rupees as a treasure since this amount will become the seed for the tree of prosperity. It is this treasure that will open further doors for you. People do not inculcate the habit of saving money or it is their parents who do not inculcate the habit of saving in them. Hence they always feel the pinch of money. Understand the secret behind growing this tree of prosperity as soon as possible.

Start paying attention to *your* money rather than others' money from today onwards. Attention is energy, a power. This power of attention will help you make money a highway to reach your destination. After all, money is only a path — a strong path but not the goal. Use money to reach your ultimate aim of enligtenment; make a blessing out of it.

Problem of money

For a man walking on the path of truth, it is of utmost importance to put money to proper use. Otherwise, most of his time is wasted in resolving worldly matters; consequently, he is not able to tread the path of truth. Many, who get involved in chasing money, never return to the path of truth, as they never feel satisfied. They do not feel they have earned enough and can now return to spirituality. They are not satisfied with the amount they possess. They always feel that whatever money they have is insufficient.

The third secret says, 'There is enough.' Now divide the money into ten portions and use the nine portions to meet all your expenditure. These nine portions should suffice for charity too. You need to accommodate all heads of expenditure that you have spent so far within these nine portions. Never think that all the heads of expenditure cannot be catered to. They can be addressed and accommodated within the nine portions of money. This will also help curtail your unwanted expenditures, which you may have been unknowingly indulging in so far.

Problem of money = wrong addictions + negligence + lethargy – understanding

Financial problems of people get solved when they get rid of their addictions, get over their carelessness, work on their indolence, shake off their lethargy and improve their understanding of money. Otherwise financial problems continue to plague you throughout your life. In order to avoid facing problems, divide your time, love and money into ten portions and keep the tenth portion aside. Assume that this one portion of money is not yours. There are people who save money and later party lavishly by using the same money. In this way, they spend the entire money on futile expenditure. Some people start saving money but when some happy occasion arises in their life, they feel like celebrating and buying something or the other. These people spend all their savings in such celebrations. Some people spend the interest they receive on their long-term savings over such parties.

People do not know how to hunt for a treasure, how to dig for it, how to build it. But when you already have a treasure, there is no need to hunt for it. The only problem is that you are not able to build it due to wrong habits or lack of understanding of money. This treasure can be built by inculcating a few useful habits.

Budget is your defence minister

Budget is your defence minister. To fulfil your highest desire (i.e. the highest and the most basic desire of your true self — self-realisation) and achieve the highest expression (of your true self), you need to safeguard yourself from trivial desires. Your trivial desires and need for comfort, convenience and safety kill your highest desire. Very often, you end up spending a lot of time in fulfilling your petty desires. As a result, your basic desire (self-realisation) remains unfulfilled as you are not left with any money, time or strength. You need to plan a budget in order to safeguard your highest desire.

A budget will become your defence minister, as it were. This means that when you plan your budget, you will come to know about the desires that can be fulfilled by the nine portions of your earnings. You will have to use the *mantra* of 'need' (N) or 'want' (W)'. When you go shopping, ask yourself whether by buying that object you would be serving your need (N) or want (W)? Do you want to buy it just because your neighbour has it, or is it really your need (N)? If it is a need, then definitely go ahead and buy it. If it is not a need, take a pause and use the formula of 'N' or 'W'. You need to safeguard your highest desire by using this formula. Otherwise, after spending your entire life, you may say, "I always longed to do certain things, but I did not get the time. I could not save enough money to fulfil those desires. Therefore those desires remained unfulfilled."

You need to decide which desires you want to fulfil. There are desires pertaining to ego (the feeling of 'I' as a separate entity) as well as desires of the truth, of the self. When the budget is ready, you will be able to fulfil these desires by distributing them in nine portions. Initially you may face problems in doing so, but soon you will see that it works out for you.

Everything (various forms of wealth) is naturally and constantly coming towards you. Earlier you were not aware (receptive) to receive them. Therefore these things could not reach you. Get rid of lethargy to achieve these things. Raise your awareness and do not avoid hard work in order to earn money. When you raise your awareness, you realise that you had never paid attention to these minute aspects and as a result, the financial problem always persisted. If you were to follow this rule, your problem would disappear.

If you have not planned your budget, you will find that you buy things catering to your wants whenever you get money. You unnecessarily spend on objects, such as clothes, footwear, cosmetics, etc., without realising how your money disappears. This is what happens with most people. Such persons are later heard to remark, "We earn a lot but fail to understand where the money is spent."

If you plan and write down your budget, then you will be able to identify these futile expenses as well as your carelessness and foolishness. You will find that you had never been alert about your budget. A planned budget will help you to meet all your expenses, besides saving some too. Apart from this, you will be able to donate some to charity too and thus sow the seeds of faith.

Magic-box

Prepare your budget and keep track of it. Everything should be jotted down. When everything is in written form, it helps you to arrive at the right budget and fulfil all your desires with the nine portions of your earnings. You have kept aside one portion for yourself in the form of your savings. Despite fixing your budget, if your desires are not getting fulfilled, make a magic-box for them. Stick the following label on the magic box: 'I expect miracles daily'. Drop all the unfulfilled desires written on a piece of paper into the magic-box.

Once you follow these guidelines, you will see that the tree of prosperity continues to grow, your saving potential increases and your principal amount fetches more money (interest). You are not to spend that extra money (interest) which has come to you. Because if you spend this extra money, the tree of prosperity will never grow. If you follow this rule with consistency and faith, all your money-related problems will disappear and you will be able to find the opportunity which will bring good fortune to you. Otherwise you may get caught in the cycle of fate and say wrong things, such as: *'If we are destined to attain wealth, it will come to us. Else it will not.'*

Growth of money

The next step is the growth of money. How to grow money? Every month accumulate a portion out of ten from your income. Invest this money properly by seeking the advice of experts. Invest it in such a way that it continues to grow. Stagnant water smells foul, whereas flowing water is always fresh, clean and keeps increasing. Similarly the money, which lies stagnant, becomes a block (obstruction). Therefore money needs to be grown in a proper way.

Money grows with expert advice. Money should be properly utilised so that it grows. Never get trapped in fake schemes in which people tell you that your money will increase ten or twenty times in a stipulated period. Many people are deceived by such schemes and end up losing their money. When their hard-earned money is lost, they repent throughout their life. Therefore, be careful; do not get lured by the temptation of making it overnight. Always consult the right people and invest your money as per their advice in the right avenues.

People do not respect knowledge

Suppose two parcels are kept on a table — one contains one lakh rupees (a hundred thousand) and the other contains a book. The book provides guidance on how money can grow in life and how money should be utilised. Some persons were asked to choose one of the parcels. Ninety-nine per cent of the people preferred to take the parcel containing one lakh rupees. Within a few months' time most of them were left penniless since they lacked the understanding required to make a proper utilisation of money. We fail to give importance to knowledge and understanding.

Identify the opportunity and train your thought process

People are not able to think much as their thinking has not received any training. If they are trained on this aspect, they are able to nurture their abilities. To inculcate competence implies learning new languages, new skills. Thinking about how to provide better service in your job or business is another way of becoming proficient. Money will come to you only when you improve your abilities. Therefore you need to work on improving your capability and capacity, rather than relying on fate.

In order to improve your abilities, you should awaken within yourself the wisdom to take decisions. The skill of identifying opportunities needs to be learnt, as it is the opportunity that brings you good fortune. Otherwise one keeps cribbing in the name of fate, envying someone who is supposedly lucky as he has lots of money, whilst blaming his own stars.

The goddess of wealth demands proof

The goddess of wealth (Lakshmi) is pleased with those who are cautious. She eludes those who are careless. She expects evidence from people in order to understand whether they can take care of money or not. She goes to those who are able to provide her with such evidence. If you are able to safeguard some money, she feels confident that if you are given more money, you will be able to handle it.

Usually people fall into two extremes — some people are misers who hoard money, making money their master; whereas, some squander money in futile pursuits. Without getting into either extremes, treat the money you possess as God's wealth kept in your custody, and divide it into ten portions. Save one portion for yourself and invest it appropriately so that it grows continuously. If you have understood this fact, then the goddess of wealth will be pleased with you. Do not waste whatever money you have earned on parties and feigning false grandeur. Always safeguard your money.

When the goddess of wealth is pleased with you, you are not reminded of money. She eludes those who constantly think about and hanker after her, despite being billionaires. When those, with whom the goddess of wealth is pleased, face financial constraints, they are blessed with money from some quarter at the correct time. Therefore, offer the right prayer to the goddess of wealth with devotion and always entertain thoughts of opulence (divinity). The right prayer is that you should be blessed enough so as not to remember her (money) all the time and that she should come to you even before you think of her. In addition, the goddess of wealth should bring the understanding of truth along with her (Lakshmi-Narayana) so that you do not develop ego due to wealth, but are able to make the right use of money.

Money is a blessing; do not make it a curse

Always focus on the right thing when you plan your budget. Keep one portion aside in advance; if you do that, you will see that everything else fits within your budget. You will be able to enjoy life and the creation of God called money. It is a wonderful creative mechanism. You will be able to understand how the world functions and how people are able to trade with each other easily. Money has been created to facilitate transactions between people. With this understanding, treat money as a blessing and not a curse. After earning plenty of money, some people become egoistic. This way, the blessing turns into a curse for them. Always be careful that money does not become a curse for you. After acquiring money, if you egoistically start harming and troubling others, it is wrong. This way, you are inculcating a bad habit for which you will have to pay a heavy price in the long run. Keep away from such vices and remember, you have to repay all your outstanding debts. Debts create blocks (obstructions) in the money flow coming towards you. Avoid such money blocks. If you have borrowed money, then ensure that you repay the debt. For any reason, if you are not able to return the debt at present, then you ought to inform the lender, saying, "I want to repay you; please give me a little time, encouragement and courage."

Upon hearing these words, the lender will become happy as he might have lost all hope of getting his money back from you. However, when he realises that you genuinely want to return his debt, he will support you; perhaps, he may even lend you additional capital so as to help you progress in your trade. Do not think that you have to keep avoiding your creditors. Speak to them and assure them that you genuinely want to return their money, that you do not want to create a money block in your life by not repaying them, and that you need some time and courage.

The aim of acquiring love, money, the highest form of meditation and God can bring the highest expression, Divine devotion and supreme happiness into your life.

Chapter Three

The Wealth of Time

The Proper Use of Time

From the third secret you gain a very significant fact that your expenditure can be adjusted within any portion of your income that you want to. In the same way, your tasks too get completed within the fixed time that you decide on. For instance, if you aim to complete a given task in ten days, then consider from the beginning that you have only nine days at your disposal. Do not think that you have ten days to conclude the task. When you assume that you have only nine days for it, you find your task accomplished well within the limit. Man tends to complete his work in whatever time is allotted to him. Once a person was asked to write a book on some subject. He was provided with audio-cassettes as the material for the book. If he is given a month to complete this task, he completes it within no less than a month. When another person was asked to produce the same book within a week, he was able to complete it within one week. How was this possible?

Different people take different periods of time to complete the same task. The secret behind this is that man can complete his tasks within the time limits (deadlines) assigned to him. Man is flexible; he can survive in the higher altitudes of the Himalayas as well as endure the scorching heat of the desert of Sahara. The human being is an exceptional creation; if he so decides, he can accomplish anything in the world. He resorts to excuses as long as he does not determinedly resolve to complete a task, or as long as he is able to find a pretext to blame an external factor or other people.

Do creative things in your free time

This secret says that after completing all the assigned tasks in nine days, use the remaining tenth day for self-development or to do something creative. It is this one day that will be the cause of your progress. The inventions of this world have indeed been accomplished in such free time. When Archimedes was in the bathtub, such thoughts emerged in his mind in that free time that they became the basis for significant inventions in the history of science.

Today, the time that you give to yourself for reading this book will lead to miracles in your life. The rule about time is similar to the one which you read regarding money in the preceding chapters. You have to enforce this rule for yourself, so that you can decide and know at the outset the amount of time available at your disposal.

For instance, if there are a hundred days left for your examination, tell yourself that you have only ninety days. This is because you will divide those hundred days into ten portions and you will use nine portions (ninety days) for the given task, while setting aside one portion (ten days) for yourself. Your preparation during those ten days can lead to your excelling in the examination. In these ten days, you will think over something and follow it up in the examination that no other student would have done. Otherwise, you tend to devote the entire hundred days to completion of the syllabus before appearing for the examination, and not too enthusiastically at that.

Those ten days are a vital seed for your success in the examination. Setting aside a day out of the ten days is yet another vital seed for doing something creative. Setting aside ten rupees from a sum of hundred rupees at your disposal is a seed that can be of immense consequence. Therefore, never underestimate this saving of money or time. If you start working on this, you will understand the secret of prosperity and why everyone needs to follow it.

Man tends to complete his work in whatever time is allotted to him.

Chapter Four

The Wealth of Love

Give Back to the World

Learn to love yourself

Divide your wealth of love as well into ten portions and set aside one portion for yourself, because only the one who loves himself and forgives himself can forgive and love others. Otherwise it becomes very difficult for people to forgive others. One thinks, 'When I have never forgiven myself, why should I forgive others?' He feels that if he is so capable, others should also be equally competent. Therefore he never forgives others. Hence you are told to divide your wealth of love into ten parts and learn to love yourself as well.

The wealth of love is your treasure. Treat the portion of love that you set aside for yourself as your lucrative capital. Treat a portion of your attention that you set aside for yourself as your asset. Treat a portion of the funds (money) that you save for yourself as your fortune. Treat a portion of time that you save for yourself as your treasure. 'Lucrative capital', 'asset', 'fortune' and 'treasure' are different words given here just to facilitate memory, but actually they all mean the same — wealth. The word 'lucrative capital' has been given alongside 'love'. Likewise, the word 'asset' has been used with 'attention'. 'Fund' (money) has been associated with 'fortune' and the word 'treasure' is mentioned alongside 'time'. You need to accumulate these forms of wealth. Wealth in these forms will be instrumental in a big way to your progress. Under the pretext of various problems, you always keep away from knowing the final truth or do not give it due importance. You should divide these forms of wealth in ten portions, fit your budget within nine portions and set aside one portion for yourself. You will find that everything gets accommodated within these nine portions; you only need to plan your budget of money, time, love and attention.

Debt owed to the world and bright (*tej*) love

After clearing all kinds of debts, you need to free yourself from the debt you owe to the world. It is only when you relate to all objects and beings in the world out of unconditional, unremitting and unlimited love (*tej* or bright love) that you are able to repay your debt to the world. When you abound in bright love towards all objects and beings in the world, then you can take it that you are liberated from the dues owed to the world. When children become instrumental in leading their parents to tread the path of truth, they get liberated from their debt to their parents. If you wish to be free from the debt you owe to the Earth, then your relationship with everyone should be built on bright love. What needs to be understood is that as long as you harbour hatred towards even a single person, be it your boss, your neighbour or an old enemy, your debt continues. Pray to God for time and courage so as to be free from this debt at the earliest.

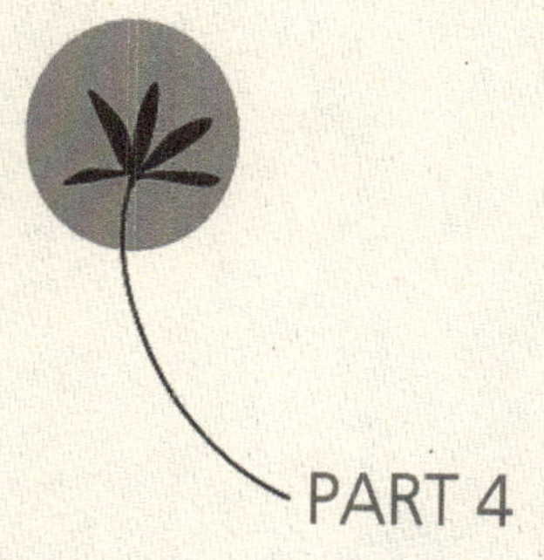

PART 4

Fourth Supreme Secret of Life

Chapter One

The Fourth Supreme Secret of Life

The Left Door in the House of the Supreme

The fourth supreme secret of life says: *'Whenever and whatever you get in your life is your necessity at that moment. What comes to you is exactly what you need at that particular point of time.'*

The meaning of this mysterious secret is that what happens with you right now is your necessity at this moment. Suppose you attend a programme and do not get a place to sit in the hall. You are made to sit somewhere outside and shown the programme on LCD. Then according to the fourth supreme secret, this is exactly what you need at that time!

The mind will not accept this. It will feel, 'How can this be my necessity? This was not what I needed at all.' But when you understand this secret in all its aspects, then you say, 'Indeed, all arrangements have been made for my progress and according to my prayers. At that time I did not feel that was my need. In ignorance I did not know what is my need.' Look around in all directions to find what is happening with you at this moment. Look at it in accordance with the fourth supreme secret. 'What is happening is my need at this time' — this form of thinking will change your point of view. This does not imply that you should not try to change the circumstances. As soon as you understand the fourth secret in depth, you get stabilised in the present moment with a feeling of acceptance.

If you ask, 'I am getting a bad cough at this moment, is it necessary?' The answer is 'Yes. Cough is an indication that you have to take care of your health now to be able to express yourself fully in the future.' A small indication can alert you, provided you are ready to look at your need. If you do not accept this secret to be the truth, then you would resist what happens at present. This resistance would only lead to depression and ignorance, spoiling your present which becomes beautiful on achieving understanding of the fourth secret.

The fact is that man does not know what is his need. When he goes to listen to the truth in a discourse, the first thing he asks is, "Tell me what all is going to happen." At that time he is told, "You will be guided here in the right way. Step by step you will get whatever you need (in accordance with the fourth supreme secret). It is crucial that certain things are not known beforehand." If that person is honest and interested in receiving guidance (i.e. if he is open-minded), he will receive the truth that is coming every moment to each one of us.

The mind of man always desires to wander into the past or the future. The funeral pyre of man gets prepared due to worries about the future. Yet people keep running behind astrologers to know what would occur in future. Astrologers will never tell you that it is extremely important not to know some things beforehand. This is because predicting the future is their business and the source of their livelihood. They would never want you to come out of their web and attain freedom. They would want to make you a fatalist (one who believes that he is powerless to change his fate or destiny) and imprison you in the cycle of joys and sorrows. If you want to attain freedom from this prison, don't change your destiny, but change your perspective.

Don't postpone living your life

People are not able to live life at all. They live either in the past or in the future. Life is not in the past or the future; it is in the present. Many people keep postponing living their life and say, "We will live life later; first let us earn something — to eat and travel." This way they spend their entire life without knowing the secrets of life. They are unable to live in the present. Their mind keeps running to some place where there is no truth, no present. Their attention is never on the present. The fourth secret always manages to bring you in the present. Let us understand the fourth secret in depth in the next chapter.

Which truth do you want — the actual truth or that truth which your mind likes?

Chapter Two

The Fourth Secret, a New Perspective – 'This is That'

Don't Agree or Disagree; Just Know

Through this book you have to make a journey through supreme bliss, supreme life and supreme silence. For the preparation of this journey you are being explained the five supreme secrets of life and *mantras*. The *mantra* associated with the fourth secret is: *'This is that what I need.'*

You have been shown below the symbol of a bracket made with the help of a hand. You have to put that situation which has appeared in your life within the brackets. 'This is that what I need' — a clap or maybe a slap. In order to view any event that occurs in your life from the right perspective, you have to put that event within this bracket. Make a symbol of a bracket with your hand as shown in the picture and repeat the *mantra*, 'This is that what I need at this moment.' In short you can say, 'This is *that*.' The other person may not give a good response, there may be a traffic jam, your shoes may get stolen from outside the temple — all such incidents will fall within the brackets. For every incident, you will say, 'Whatever happens now is what I need.'

'This is that' is a small but powerful *mantra*. On using this *mantra* you will become aware of the present and be ready to learn. Your perspective and attitude will change completely upon using this *mantra*. Suppose you wake up in the morning and find there is a power cut. You say, 'This is that what I need.' You would repeat this *mantra* even though you do not know whether you really need it. Your mind does not accept it, but you will say, 'My mind does not agree, but this is the truth.' The sooner your mind accepts and understands the truth, the sooner will it attain bliss. It is up to you to decide how long you want to postpone your happiness. You can attain the state of bliss here and now, provided you have the understanding of the five supreme secrets of life.

When you put every incident, every situation and every problem within the brackets, everything changes. As long as that incident or problem is outside the brackets, it keeps troubling you. When it comes within the brackets, it gets accepted through right understanding. This is the miracle of the bracket. As soon as you say, 'This is that what I need' after a situation arises, your attitude towards that situation changes.

Instead of repeating the full sentence, you can just put the entire understanding within a small *mantra* and say, 'This is *that*.' The full *mantra* is 'This is that what I need.'

A saint was passing through a village with his disciples. His disciples said, "It's getting late and it will be dark by the time we reach the next village. Let us stay here for the night."

The saint replied, "No, we will proceed further."

The disciples could not oppose him and they all set off for the next village. It was indeed night time when they reached there. The majority of people were those who belonged to a different sect. They were quite unwelcoming and did not provide any accommodation to them. They gave them neither food nor a place to stay. The disciples were upset as they had not wished to be there in the first place.

They started complaining, "We had told you that we should have stayed in the previous village. We shouldn't have come to this place. Where will we go at this hour of the night?"

The saint answered, "Don't jump to conclusions. Just see whatever is happening."

If those disciples had known the *mantra*, they would have said, 'This is that what we need.' But they did not know this *mantra*; hence, they couldn't say it and continued to feel despondent.

They found a ramshackle hut outside the village to spend the night. Half the roof was missing and the walls were ready to crumble. The disciples slept with a troubled mind in that dilapidated place. When night set in, what a night it was! A lovely full moon shone in the sky in all its glory! When the saint opened his eyes after midnight, he witnessed that breathtaking view in the sky. He was moved to ecstasy. He then woke up his disciples, saying, "Wake up and look at this amazing spectacle in the sky!" When the disciples viewed the marvellous scene, they were overwhelmed and transported to a state of bliss and *samadhi*. This is when they realised that had they not come to the place, they would not have experienced that state of bliss and *samadhi*.

Thus the disciples accepted, "This is that what we need. Every incident that happens to us is our necessity."

The saint might have used different words to explain the fourth secret to his disciples, but the meaning would have been the same. This story thus explains, 'This is that what I need.' It happens a lot of times that when an incident occurs, you feel it is wrong and that you certainly don't need it. Those disciples too felt the same way. But when the next scene appeared, it became evident as to what they were being prepared for, what kind of experience they were to attain, and what was the next scene on account of which this scene was created. The one who sees from a higher perspective (helicopter view) is able to understand, 'this is that what I need.'

Let us take up some more examples. Suppose you are not satisfied with your present job and pray, "O God! Give me a bigger better job." After some days, your boss fires you. At such time, can you say,

'This is that what I need?' On the contrary, you are shocked — you had prayed for a better job but you lose even what you have. You lose faith in your prayer. You start searching for another job and find that there is a vacancy in a good firm where those not employed elsewhere can apply. You get the job. Now you discover that being fired from your old job was your necessity; otherwise how could you have got the bigger and better job? The first scene was a preparation for the next scene.

A man is in dire need of money. He prays for it with all his heart. Suddenly, an earthquake occurs and the walls of his house start shaking. He gets scared and his faith starts to waver. He had prayed for money but here he finds that he is about to lose even his house. He stops praying. Had he been convinced of, 'this is that what I need,' he would have realised that this was the way his prayer was being answered, since his ancestors had hidden a treasure in one of the walls of the house!

A little boy is caught in a maze. There are many different paths winding and meandering in it. He takes a wrong path from which there is no way out. While walking, he gets slapped by an unknown hand from the other side. Deeply upset and scared, he turns towards another path. He gets slapped again. This happens many times. When slapped, he is unable to say, 'This is *that*.' But when he takes the right path and comes out of the maze, he says, "Oh! All those slaps were for steering me in the right direction! I needed those slaps!!"

However, while being slapped, if he were asked, "Do you feel this is what you need?", he would not have agreed.

If you conduct a survey, you will find that due to ignorance, people are not able to accept the events occurring in their lives and live in constant misery. In such a situation, what is needed is courage that arises from understanding. It is required to tread the path of truth, but truth appears illogical to the mind. When the mind does not accept that this incident is what you need, then tell your mind, 'This is exactly what I need.'

Let us assume that a situation arises where somebody steals your idea and touts it as his own. He gets full credit for it and the resultant fame and success. At such times too, remember to say, 'This is what I need.' Your mind may retort, 'I simply cannot accept that this is what I need.' However, the mind does not know what the future has in store for you. The truth is that whatever is happening with you at this moment is for your progress and development.

Don't accept the secret, just know it

The body in which new, fresh and creative ideas appear has some quality — it has receptivity for new ideas and thoughts. Thoughts pass through the body, but are not generated by the body. Thoughts arise from all sides. The one (God) who gives the thoughts sees which body is transparent, deceit-free, appropriate and capable of receiving creative thoughts. If you have this understanding, you will say, 'This is that what I need', even when somebody steals your idea. This is because the source of thoughts is within you and it cannot be stolen. Hence, you will have no problems with that situation. Your mind will say, 'I don't agree.' Tell your mind, 'Don't agree or disagree; just know it.' Also tell your mind, 'No one is asking you to agree.' This means that you don't have to agree, nor do you have to disagree. You just have to know. Once you know this truth, this fourth secret, there will be no need to agree. Until you don't know this secret, you have to agree because you have to begin somewhere. Therefore, tell your mind right now, 'Don't get into this cycle of agreement and disagreement; just know it because it *is* the truth. After the present incident has taken place, become aware at least on seeing the next scene that appears.' When you tell your mind this, it will become patient and begin to witness the process of problems getting solved. This perspective is essential for the mind. Due to this new perspective, maturity, tolerance, receptivity for the truth and purity develop in the mind. Then the mind does not run behind astrologers to change its fate; it will learn to change its attitude. Don't change your fate; change your perspective.

Whenever and whatever you need, you get it. Whatever happens with you at this time is your need and necessity. It may not be essential for someone else, but it is definitely essential for you. This book in your hand right now may or may not be useful for someone else, but is extremely crucial for you. People look at others and reject the knowledge that comes to them. They think, 'Others are not reading this book, then why should I? Others are not doing this, why should I?' However, you have to understand that everybody's *Gita* or story is different. According to your story, you are building a path. The guidance you receive is perfect for you. All the things that happen in your life are there to help you build your path. If you move ahead with this understanding, you would not be disturbed by any incident in your life.

Whatever is happening right now
is exactly what you need at this moment
because every scene is a preparation for the next scene.

Chapter Three

Look at Depression from a New Angle

'Can I Convert the Snakes into Ladders?'

The next step after accepting a given situation is to ask, "Can I convert it (whatever is happening) into a ladder?" This means that whatever incident has occurred, can you convert it into a ladder, a stepping-stone? Can you use it for your progress? Can you use it for your all-round self-development?

In the classical board-game of snakes and ladders, you go up the ladder and come down a snake. However, you should learn to transform every snake into a ladder and every obstacle into an instrument for growth. In every adverse situation, ask yourself, 'Can I turn the snakes into ladders?' You will be astonished to learn that actually every snake can be converted into a ladder. This is exactly what spiritualism teaches you.

It says, "The world is a game of snakes and ladders and spiritualism is the knowledge of converting snakes into ladders." To convert snakes into ladders means that you should learn how to successfully use any negative incident that occurs in your life or a negative thought that arises in the mind. You may accept it, but that is just the first step. There is one more step — learn something from that incident. This will help you attain your goal of progress, success and happiness. Progress signifies the knowledge of converting snakes into ladders. The snakes in our life are depression, stress, worry, anger and the like that prevent us from achieving true happiness. These can be converted into ladders to attain happiness.

When people are depressed and sad in life, they cry out, 'Why am I depressed?' They should, in fact, be congratulated. Why? Because those who get depressed are the ones who become seekers later in life. When you seek and research, you come to know that depression makes you progress in life. Due to depression and sorrow, you try to find out the ultimate truth. Why do we become sad and miserable? What is the reason? Can we change our perspective? Is there something permanent and steady within us? Where should we look for it? In what perspective should we look at life? Questions like these can initiate your quest for the truth.

Do not get scared when depression sets in. You are depressed and you worry about why you are depressed, i.e. depression upon depression. That is wrong. Some people, when they feel angry, get more furious, thinking, 'Why did I get angry? I shouldn't have got angry...' They should then be pacified by saying, "It's okay to be angry, it's alright; but anger upon anger is very harmful." If you just understand that you do not have to get angry over your anger or depressed upon your depression, you will be saved from a lot of agony. If depression does set in, just see what it will do, where it will take you. It has definitely come to make you do something, which is essential for your growth. Later in life, you will say, 'It's good that I got depressed. It is due to depression that I have progressed in life.' Those who never get distressed or depressed, never achieve anything great in life. They always remain mediocre. Therefore, do not consider depression or sorrow as something bad; instead, make it a ladder for achieving final success in life (enlightenment).

Thus when any event occurs, you have to use the fourth secret,

'This is what I need.' Then you have to accept that situation. You don't have to stop at that. After accepting, you have to convert that situation into a ladder.

Those who never get distressed or depressed, never achieve anything great in life.

Chapter Four

Apply Commonsense with Acceptance

Training for Awareness

The understanding, the bitter or sweet external experiences in the world, the inner experience and the bright '*knowlerience*' (final knowledge arising from inner experience) are your necessities. The present is your necessity. What you have got in the present is your need, else you will get stuck at the windows of yesterday or tomorrow and never pay any attention to the present. That is why it is important to meditate on the present, i.e. practise 'present meditation'. 'Present meditation' brings you in the present, liberating you from the past and future. In this meditation, you have to look around to see what is awe-inspiring and thereby instantly come to the present. It can be anything — the fan, the bulb, the lift, a mosquito, an ant, your breath, a flower, the sun — just anything. Everything is miraculous, provided you look at it with that kind of eye — the eye of a child. Everything is fascinating for a child and hence a child is always in the present. Likewise, you have to look at things around and come to the present.

Do make use of commonsense

The fourth secret tells you how to look at situations in life. Do make use of commonsense when applying anything in your life. Suppose your shoes get stolen from outside a temple, and you say, "This is that what I need." Having said that, you are not told to avoid searching for your shoes. You will definitely take corrective action and put in all efforts that are necessary to search for recovering your shoes. You will give the appropriate response to the situation. As soon as you repeat the *mantra* within ('This is that what I need'), a feeling of acceptance engulfs you. Now the task at hand will be done with all your intelligence, a free and sharp intellect. It may then strike you that someone has put on your shoes by mistake. Otherwise, the brain loaded with stress cannot even think right. Therefore, you have to understand the complete and correct meaning of what is being told and also how to apply it by using your commonsense.

If someone is told, "You should speak in a soft voice," he ought to use his commonsense. This means that if he has to call someone who is far away, he would need to raise his voice. If you call a person who is far away in a low voice, he would not be able to hear you. That is why it is essential to use commonsense. After having accepted and put in brackets a given situation, it is imperative to give the appropriate response.

When you are recommended to apply the knowledge being given here to life, it definitely does not mean that you have to accept the situation and then sit with folded hands. This is what happens in spirituality. When people are told one thing, they do not understand it in totality and hold on to something different. Those, who do not want to study or work, use any situation to make some excuse. Those who want to run away from responsibilities use even the truth as an excuse. Thinking themselves to be wise, they use words of wisdom to justify their laziness. People use opium and other drugs and try to justify it by saying that such-and-such saint had also used them. Had that saint known that later on people would be using his name for indulging in such activities, he would have told them the reason in advance or quit consuming it. People are not aware as to why that saint used some drug; instead, they just find an excuse to use drugs in the name of spirituality and imitate that single action of the saint. They never copy other great actions of that saint. They then continue to lead their lives in an illusion.

Ask yourself honestly whether you want to walk the path of truth or use the truth as an excuse. Those who use the truth as an excuse to carry on with their bad habits are the ones who corrupt the truth. The Buddha preached some things, but people corrupted his teachings and practised them according to their own whims. That which was never told by the Buddha, Mahavira or other great saints was practised by some people because these people had nothing to do with the truth. They just needed the words of truth for conveniently and safely perpetuating their ego and their tendencies. Therefore, when you tread the path of truth, when you use the *mantra* of truth, ask yourself honestly whether you are doing it because you really want to walk the path of truth or you just want to cover up for your laziness or other tendencies? Only after contemplating on this question, choose the path of truth. Also, do make use of commonsense on the path of truth. You will thereby become aware and conscious.

Chapter Five

How to Use the Mantra 'This is That'

Copy Faith

You wait for the lift and the lift does not come. You repeat the fourth secret, 'This is what I need.' Until the lift arrives, you can practise the 'present meditation'. You can look around to see what is awe-inspiring and instantly come to the present, else the mind would keep chasing either the past or the future. A man prays, "O God! Give me patience." He then goes to his office, waits for the lift but the lift does not arrive. He gets irritated. He does not realise that this is the answer to his prayer. Whenever you wait in a queue, be it for ration, for tickets, for payment of bills, tell yourself, 'I had prayed for patience; this is the arrangement for it.' In what a beautiful manner your prayers get fulfilled! But if someone does not know this secret of prayer, and straightaway you tell him that whatever happens to him is his need and also the answer to his prayers, he will get upset with you.

If you want to develop patience, certain events will occur for making you patient. Otherwise what do you expect will happen when you pray for patience? Will flowers be showered on you from the heavens and will you develop patience in an instant? That is not the way it will happen. Whatever prayers you offer, such as, 'O God! I want courage', then some particular incident will occur for the same. Perhaps, someone will come and frighten you. In such a situation, you will say, 'This incident will help me develop courage. This is what I need (This is *that*).' When you get such thoughts, you will then take that situation as a challenge and find the courage you need. But if you forget this secret at that time, you will feel miserable. Waves of fear will agitate you so much that your blood pressure would rise, things will get messed up and you may fall sick. In this way you totally forget that this incident has occurred due to your prayer. Just imagine how man's life would be if he knew all the secrets of life. The one who knows the secrets and has complete faith in them will find his life simply wonderful.

Strong faith should be copied

How easily Jesus went on the cross! What was the understanding he had? Such an understanding you have to attain. You should seek inspiration from the unwavering faith that he had. Many a times people copy external things. They copy the external attributes of movie stars, but not the confidence and the conviction that is present within them. You should get that confidence and conviction. You should develop the faith which Jesus had. In whichever field you want to progress, you should copy the conviction of the successful people in that field. The ones who have self-confidence and devotion have a high level of conviction in devotion and love. Let us pray to get that kind of conviction.

This *mantra*, this secret and this understanding is given to you in order to open you up, to remove the constrictions within you and to make you see each event in a proper perspective. You have to see with the fourth eye. Till now you had been looking at incidents in a particular way, but now, after knowing this secret, your attitude will change. Henceforth, whenever an incident will take place in life, you would remind yourself to look at it with a different attitude.

Response to the present

You are going someplace and there is a traffic jam or the road is blocked. How irritated you get! And when someone overtakes you from the side, you curse him! But now that you have understood the secret, you would say, 'This is what I need.' When you have the understanding, you will say, 'This incident has occurred to teach me something.' Later on, if you happen to meet that person who overtook you on the road ahead, you would thank him because he gave you an opportunity to apply your understanding and develop patience in yourself. It is not necessary that he understands the reason for your thanking him. At least, you can thank him in your mind immediately after the incident.

If someone drops and breaks an article of yours, you get furious. However, when you remember the fourth secret, then you would first repeat the *mantra* and then see if it is possible to repair the broken article. Do think about what is the appropriate response to the situation. Do think as to what can be done for making amends. However, as soon as an incident occurs, first say, 'This is that' and after remembering the fourth secret, go ahead with an open mind. Many people come to this Earth and go away having collected thousands of antique pieces; so what happens to these objects in their absence? People get distressed if even a small object breaks accidentally and become emotional. "My greeting card... my gift which my late friend had given me... my antique piece..." This way they fight over such things with others — others who are living, conscious people. People weep over those who lived yesterday and quarrel with those who are living today. What is important is to give the right response to those who are there with us at present.

In this way, even small incidents can perform big miracles for you.

Chapter Six

Don't Change Your Fortune, Change Your Attitude

The Magic of a New Attitude

The guests living in the House of the Supreme are very lucky. Each and everything teaches us the secrets of life. The floor (chess) of the house reminds us of the first secret. The three windows inspire us to stay in the present (second secret). The open door on the right reveals the third secret. The closed door on the left teaches us how to use the fourth secret. The roof of the house demonstrates the fifth supreme secret of life. The person who comes to know all these five supreme secrets is fortunate. Does he need to change his fortune? Come, let us change our attitude, not our fortune.

New attitude towards problems

The problems in our life are not there to make us miserable. They have been given to us to teach us our lessons and also to connect with God. Otherwise, we can never connect with God. Just think what happens with those who have wealth, property, status, a good job and everything else. After having achieved everything, how far do they remember God? And there is another person who does not have much money, is searching for a job and has lots of problems; how much does he remember the Lord? Which of the two are closer to God? Who is the lucky one? If man does not have money or a job and he begins to work according to God's command to achieve these things, then he is fortunate indeed. If you forget God while having everything, there cannot be a greater loss. If your job is your boss and money your God, when you start worshipping wealth and it becomes your source, then it becomes a great blunder.

If you have problems and difficulties, do not assume that you are not fortunate. If you use these difficulties to get closer to God, then this difficulty will become instrumental in making you reach the Lord. It is during times of difficulties that the seed of faith is sown in order to go closer to God and to know his way of working. You will say, 'It's good that this problem came to the fore ('this is *that*'), due to which I learnt the ways of the Lord.'

Those people are most fortunate who have money, job and other things and do not forget God. They use that money for the highest expression of the true self and for fulfilment of the desire of God. How can you become fortunate and most fortunate? It is possible to attain freedom from fate and become 'bright lucky'. The word 'bright' means that 'which is beyond the two polarities'. It means beyond *karma* (your deeds) and destiny.

Power of acceptance

Acceptance has incredible power. When everything is accepted, be it the prick of a needle or your neighbour's shiny new car, it's then that you derive the joy of acceptance. This does not mean in any way that now that you have accepted, you don't have to aspire for a car or a bungalow. It is being said that whatever is there, first accept it as it is. Whatever face or body you have got, first accept it. Whatever be your state, first accept it and remember 'This is what I need.' Do not think, 'Alas! If only my height had been more... I wish I had been born in that family... I wish I were born in that country... I wish that big politician was my acquaintance...' Whatever is the situation, it should be accepted as it is. As soon as you accept it, your hands become free. If you don't accept, it means you tie one hand behind your back and try to solve the problem with just one free hand. The problem does not get solved easily with one hand. As soon as you say, 'I accept it,' your hands become free and all problems are solved easily.

Let us understand this with the help of an example. There is a machine which runs at a speed of 80 mph. It desires to run at the speed of 90 mph. It tries to run at the speed of 90 mph, but is unable to do so. It gets stressed, thinking, 'Why am I like this? Why am I not able to move ahead fast? Why does this always happen with me?' In this way, every incident or situation is unacceptable to this machine. It feels such things should not happen with it. As soon as such feelings develop in it, its speed falls to 75 mph. One day when it listens to the secrets of life, it learns that no matter what the speed is, it should be accepted. When it accepts everything, its speed returns to 80 mph and continues so for some days. Then suddenly one day its speed increases to 85 mph. The acceptance works like a lubricant for it. Acceptance is an oil that enters your machine and increases its power. Initially you will feel that although you have accepted, things are not turning out your way, but as you go on accepting, suddenly you will begin to realise the method of working of the Supreme and the supreme secrets of the Supreme.

God works through relaxed bodies (those who have the feeling of acceptance) that express without any stress or tension. For instance, when somebody gives a dance performance on stage, he leaves his body completely relaxed. When the body is not tense (stress-free), only then is he able to dance well and express himself well. The body in which there is tension will think, 'What if I goof up! What if people boo me?' If such a fear enters the mind, then God will not be able to express himself through that body. People say, "I started dancing and I don't know what happened! I never knew that I could dance so well; how did this happen?" A musician says, "I was so lost while playing that I didn't realise how the music was going on and who was playing it!" This means God wants to work through the body of man but the ego (the feeling of being a separate entity) of man becomes the obstacle. As soon as man surrenders to God and starts accepting, God begins to carry out his work.

Who is lucky?

Those who have wealth, are they lucky? Or, are those ones lucky in whose horoscope it is written: 'You will gain wealth'?

A man who earns ten million rupees a year calls himself lucky. The second year he gets a promotion and earns twenty million rupees a year and thus feels very happy. The third year he earns fifteen million rupees and feels unhappy. He begins to feel very unfortunate. He does not understand that there was once a time when he was earning ten million and felt very lucky. But because his earnings in the third year were less in comparison to the second year, he feels sad because the belief has taken root in his mind that his earnings ought to increase every year. There is nothing fixed about money; you never know when it will dwindle. There is ignorance about money in people, which can be removed by understanding the truth.

Once Guru Nanak (the founder of the Sikh religion) went to a village. The custom in that village was that whoever had one lakh (a hundred thousand) rupees, was given a flag to put up on his house. There were five such flags waving over the house of a particular person. That person told Guru Nanak, "I have so much wealth that I am worried about how I will take it when I go to the other world after death. Please tell me some solution for the same."

Guru Nanak gave him a needle and said, "Keep this needle with you and return it to me when I meet you in the other world. I will then give you your wealth there."

This person became happy, thinking what a simple solution he had got. He went home and told his wife excitedly, "Look, what an easy method I found to take my wealth with me in the next world!"

Hearing it, his wife replied, "Hey! You haven't understood the matter. The guru indicated something to you and you did not comprehend it. After your death, your body will be cremated here, then how will you go to the other world with a needle? The one who told you such a profound thing must be a wise man indeed."

The rich person understood and decided, 'If we are not capable of taking even a needle with us, then how can we take our entire wealth with us after our death? The wealth of consciousness is the only treasure which we can take along with us to the next world.'

Having gained this insight, the rich man realised his folly. He understood that wealth and status would not remain with him till the end; it's then that his focus shifted from money. Thoughts start arising in his mind that there is something other than wealth, besides money, which has to be attained. Those who have attained the wealth of consciousness, courage, love, health and meditation are the real fortunate ones. Due to this wealth, money is attracted towards you and you get it easily. *Are those people lucky who have a luxurious bed but no sleep; wealth but no health?* That man is lucky who has attained complete knowledge (supreme secrets of life) and thus is liberated from destiny.

Those who have political power should be asked if they are fortunate. You will get astonishing answers. They will say, "We are always worried that we have attained this position now but what will happen after the next elections? The government changes after a certain period, thousands of people have their eyes fixed upon this post and the tension keeps on mounting. When there was no post, there was no tension; but once this post is obtained, it is difficult to maintain it and hang on to it." It is easy for them to achieve a position but very difficult to hold on to it because the position and power are an attraction for many. Hence it cannot be said that you are lucky if you have attained power and position. On the contrary, people in power are plagued much more by insecurity about the future.

Can someone be called lucky on account of possessing physical strength? Duryodhana (a character in the great Indian epic, *Mahabharata*) was physically very strong, had power, a grand palace, great wealth, but he always burned in the fire of his ego and kept on plotting against his cousins to avenge them. His strength did not prove to be an asset for him. Even today people remember him as a bad warrior, a bad character.

If a film star is asked whether he feels blessed, what will his answer be? If he answers honestly, he will say, "I am very stressed; wrinkles are increasing on my face, I don't know if I'll get roles in the future or not. Today people adore me, but what if they reject me tomorrow!"

If all those people mentioned above, such as the wealthy, powerful, strong, famous and beautiful are not fortunate, then who is fortunate? A strict physical instructor of a school was teaching the students about road accidents as well as telling them the rules to be followed on the road. He asked one of the students, "What is the difference between an accident and bad luck?"

The kid replied, "Sir, if you are crossing the road and if you are hit by a car, then it's an accident. And if you survive that accident, then it's your bad luck." You can understand that this teacher must be scolding the children very often. According to the understanding of children, the one who is not scolded is lucky. This implies that it's bad luck for the one who receives punishment and it's good luck for the one who gets praised. Then, is this the appropriate definition of good luck and bad luck?

Everybody is engrossed in changing his fortune according to his own definition. We don't have to change our fate or fortune; we have to change our attitude. We don't have to change other people; we have to change our thinking. We don't have to recognise others; but recognise our self. When all these three tasks are accomplished, then we will become 'bright lucky'. The 'bright lucky' is the one who gets liberated from *karma* (deeds and their fruit) and destiny. He is the one who has stopped working, because every work of his has become the expression of self (true self). On changing your perspective about work, your actions become the expression of self; religion becomes your nature and service becomes your devotion.

Bright sun sign

Once a girl was told by an astrologer, "You will have a sudden death. This means you will either have an accident or a fall from the stairs and you will die." Now this girl began to lead her life in constant fear. Every time, while descending the stairs, she was scared that she would fall down. While walking down the street, she was afraid that she would meet with an accident. She dies a thousand deaths before her actual death. Death will arrive at its time but before that, she will live, dying every moment. This is the kind of prediction and destiny that people are stuck with.

There are nearly 6.6 billion people in the world and there are 12 sun signs, which implies that there are 458 million people under each sun sign. That means the same prediction is made for so many people. But the fact is that nobody on Earth has a future like yours. Astrologers are able to tell just one out of the several possibilities you have. Instead of getting entangled in their predictions, you should change your attitude and your thinking.

If you do want to read your horoscope in the newspaper, then read the predictions under all the sun signs and choose the one which foretells the best future. This implies that now you do not belong to just one sun sign, but you are the one to whom all the sun signs belong. Then you will look with the attitude of 'all sun signs are mine' and whatever good is going to happen under any sign, you will take it as 'that is mine.' Due to this, you will be surprised to discover how your thoughts attract events towards you. Wrong thoughts frighten you and then this fear attracts those fearful things towards itself. Then why not get freedom from destiny? Those who believe in *karma* (you get the results according to your deeds), would not agree with this, but we should get liberated from *karma* too because the one who performs deeds, his ego ('I did this') goes on increasing. Hence we have to learn to be the non-doer and express the true self (the real doer). When we get liberated from both *karma* and destiny, it is then that we will be truly lucky.

Don't be curious to know your future. The negative things that you will come to know through astrology can keep troubling your mind. Many people have spoiled their present due to this. Choose your own future. Don't remain in a cage like a bird, which wants to enter the cage even after being let out; it does not like the open sky. The reality is that we get chained to our worries, but like to talk about the open sky. If we want to touch the skies, we have to fill ourselves with positive thoughts and banish the fear of the sun signs from our mind.

You have to become the one belonging to the 13th sun sign. This means that either all the signs are yours or none is yours. This is the 'bright sun sign', which is beyond joys and sorrows, life and death, success and failure, and beyond all the twelve sun signs. People belonging to the 'bright sun sign' and bright religion know their true self. To know your true self, read the fifth supreme secret of life.

Drop the contrast mind

Once a man took some flowers to the Buddha. There were flowers with thorns in his left hand and flowers without thorns in his right hand. He planned to give the flowers from his right hand to the Buddha. When he reached there, the Buddha said, "Drop them." He dropped the flowers of the left hand since it is a belief among some of us that the left hand is impure. Again the Buddha said, "Drop them." He was baffled, thinking, 'He is telling me to drop all the flowers. I had come here thinking that I would please the Buddha with flowers and he would impart wisdom to me.' He did not realise what the Buddha was telling him to drop. He was telling him to drop the thoughts of duality in his mind, implying that he should come out of his false beliefs.

The 'contrast mind' or the mind with thoughts of duality always divides everything into two — good and bad, joys and sorrows, respect and disrespect, flowers and thorns, left and right. When the 'contrast mind' falls, only then will the true self (supreme truth), hidden by it, manifest. The one in whom the true self manifests, the one in whom the spring of eternal bliss breaks out, is the one who is truly fortunate. The one who has understanding, right thinking, right perspective, and the one who knows his true self is the one who is truly lucky.

You were not aware when you were sowing the seeds of thorns; you were not ready for contemplation at that time; but when the tree of thorns has grown out, at least then understand and contemplate so that you won't sow wrong seeds in the future.

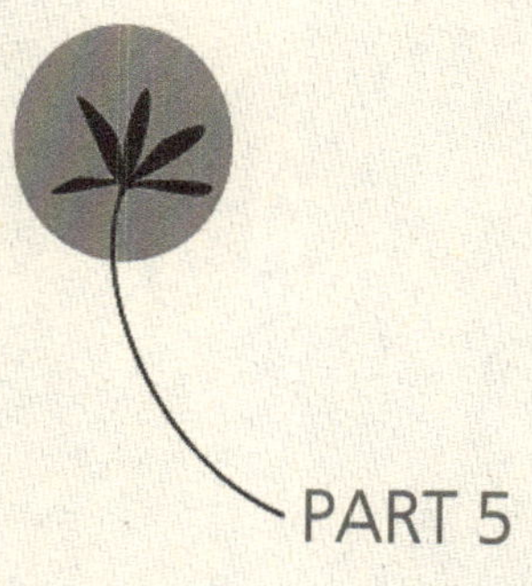

PART 5

Fifth Supreme Secret of Life

Chapter One

The Fifth Supreme Secret of Life

The Mystery of Knowledge and 'I'

After having understood the four secrets of life, let us now understand the fifth one. The fifth supreme secret of life is: *'You are with the body; you are not the body.'* This appears to be a small statement; however, when you contemplate deeply over it, you can fathom the depth of this secret.

If you are *with* the body, but not the body, then who are you? You will understand this with the aid of the fifth secret, which throws light on the true nature of your being, showing who you really are. Innumerable diverse bodies inhabit the Earth. Are these bodies separate from each other or is there something universal functioning through them? This is what the profound fifth secret of life reveals.

You are the 'real I'

It is difficult to explain who we are in words, as this is something that can only be experienced. When language was born for the first time within a human being, then which word would he have used to refer to himself? The first word in this world was created by God to refer to himself. In order to refer to himself, man used the word 'I' — the 'I' that you are in essence, in reality.

When experiential knowledge is expressed in words, it gives rise to statements, such as, "You are that 'I'." This statement appears to be strange and grammatically incorrect. However, when knowledge (of the true self) is expressed in words, then such statements are used to lead the truth-seeker to the experience of the self.

When the disciple approaches the guru with the question, "Who am I?", the Guru replies, "You are that 'I'." The disciple cannot comprehend the answer. He muses as to what kind of an answer it is. In order to understand this answer, he needs to contemplate on what could be the first word that God used. Various languages have their own equivalent words for 'I'. In reality, all these words are used to address God himself.

Expression through the medium of the human body

When man, pointing to himself, asked the question, "Who is this?", he got an answer, "This is 'I'." "I am" is verily the expression of the highest knowledge in words. 'I' is the expression of the first knowledge in words; but how is the word 'I' being used today? Today, this word has lost its original meaning; it has been contaminated. It all depends on how this word is used. If the word 'I' is used for something ignoble, it becomes inferior; whereas if it is used to indicate something higher, then it becomes superior.

When God used the word 'I' to refer to himself, it was the cause of unlimited happiness! What a time it must have been! The sole purpose why God created the world was to express himself. The human body is the only instrument that God can use to think about himself (or become aware of himself). Without the human body God cannot think. It is only the human body that is endowed with the thinking faculty. Animals are not provided with this faculty. It is only by associating with the human body that God can realise himself and his qualities.

The very purpose of the human body is to be the medium for God's expression. We have to remember this.

Chapter Two

'I', the Purest (Dissociated) Consciousness

Who is Associated with the Body?

The word 'I' is God's highest creation. God used this word to refer to himself; however, out of ignorance, man abuses even words of wisdom. The human body is that arrangement made by God that is endowed with the full potential of getting deluded as well as liberated from the delusion.

The human mechanism has both the qualities — it can get deluded as well as free itself. Thoughts can lead to delusion as well as help us to emerge out of delusion. The idols of God can either baffle us or help us understand the underlying truth. This is only possible with human beings, as only we have the potential to create heaven and hell. Animals live a natural life without any expectations. In animals, there is no concept of heaven and hell. There is a possibility of both positive as well as negative only in human beings, due to which God used the word 'I'. Those bodies through which self-realisation took place recognised that the word 'I' represents the highest wisdom.

The Hindi word for 'I' i.e. *'Mai'*, when reversed, sounds like *Aum*. The syllable *Aum* seems powerful and effective. Man appreciates such words. People have not been able to appreciate the difficulty faced by the self-realised saints in communicating the knowledge of self in words. If this knowledge is conveyed by using simple and easy words, there will be no impact on the people who will remain the same. Until and unless a special vocabulary of words is used together with apt and interesting stories, people do not meditate on the self (true 'I', *tejam*).

Chanting of the self

'Chanting of the self' implies remembering the true nature of your being beyond the body. This chant cannot be conveyed in words. When language was invented and words were used for the first time, man could attain that true state of being just by repeating the word 'I'. But today, chanting the word 'I' does not lead to that state due to its wrong identification with the body. The word 'I' reminds man only of his body and face. By repeating the word 'I', his ego gets bloated. The word 'I', which could have been the medium for liberation, may now lead to further delusion. Therefore, the word 'I' is not being used for chanting. Today, the regular mundane use of the words 'I' and *Aum* have resulted in the loss of their true significance. The need of a word has emerged in spiritualism by using which man can directly reach the original state of being.

Significance of the word *'tejam'*

Tejam means the 'I' which is beyond 'I' and you. It means the Universal Self or the true self. When you utter the word *'tejam'*, you will not associate it with your body, mind or intellect. Chanting of this word will help you reach your original state of being.

Become a bright (*tej*) believer

You must have come across words like 'atheist' and 'believer'. The atheist says, "God does not exist," while the believer says, "God exists". However, both have incomplete knowledge. You might have also seen atheists turn into believers. After many years of being a non-believer, when the atheist is faced with difficulties in life, he begins to say to God, 'If this task of mine is accomplished, then I will start trusting you.' And if he does get what he wants, he starts trusting God with full force. You might have also seen a believer become an atheist. If someone questions him about his change into an atheist, he explains that when his prayer to God was not fulfilled, he lost faith in God. What kind of faith is that? Both atheists as well as believers have incomplete knowledge. You might have seen wooden toy horses, which cannot move from one place to another; they only keep swinging back and forth at one spot. Atheists and believers can be compared to such a wooden horse.

You are *with* the body

The word 'I' does not refer to the body, mind or the intellect. It is the purest, unconditioned and dissociated consciousness. As this state of consciousness had to designated by some name, the word 'I' was originally used for this purpose. Despite being so pure and powerful, the word 'I' has become detrimental as man has forgotten the fifth secret of life.

The fifth secret of life is: *'You are with the body; you are not the body'*. When you were a toddler, you were very clear about the fact that you were not the body. Listen to the poems that children recite. They read poems like, "I am a teapot, short and stout. This is my handle..." Saying so, they place their hand on their waist.

From this poem, we can understand that the teapot has a handle; however, the handle in itself is not the teapot. The teapot also refers to the empty space in which tea is kept. This empty space is the most important part of the teapot, without which the teapot would not exist. Whenever we talk about the teapot, we do not just refer to its spout or its handle. Just as when reciting the poem, the child refers to his hand and says, "This is my handle." Likewise, you can easily say, "This is my hand; I shake hands with it. My hands are handles and my legs are paddles; I am not any of these."

If you are able to appreciate these facts as clearly as toddlers can, then how would you use your body? You will be aware and conscious when you say, 'I'. This example helps you understand that you are not the body; you are *with* the body.

The word 'I' is God's highest creation. God has used this word to refer to himself; however, out of ignorance, man tends to abuse this word of wisdom.

Chapter Three

Identify the Word 'I' with the 'Real I'

'I' Represents the Universal Self

In a lunatic asylum, all inmates indulge in insane talk and behaviour. Therefore the lunatics never perceive their fellow inmates as lunatics. When a normal person visits the asylum to present a gift, he realises that all these inmates are insane as they behave senselessly. However, these lunatic inmates regard this normal person to be crazy. If this visitor were a film star and were to say, "I am a film star," the lunatics would respond, "You will recover in a couple of days. When people arrive here, they all say what you are saying. We also used to consider ourselves as film stars, but after being given a few electric shocks, we recovered. After receiving the electric shocks, you too will recuperate. There's nothing to be worried about."

When all say the same thing, the statement does not sound silly (even if it is actually ridiculous). That is why regarding the body as 'I' does not sound absurd to you since everybody does that. Who is it within you who originally wanted to use these words? It is indeed the experience of being (self, self-witness, God) within us that created these words and wished to make use of them for itself. Instead of being used to refer to the 'real I', the word 'I' is being used to refer to the illusory individual (*maya*). Instead of being the medium for God's expression, the human body has become the instrument for expression of the ego (false 'I', which is born as a result of an assumed separation of the individual from the perceived world). In the process, the truth got hidden.

When the fifth secret is revealed, man starts taking note of, 'When do I use the word 'I'? What is the nature of this 'I'?' It is just like water. When water occupies a container, it assumes the shape of the container. In that sense, 'I' is akin to water, since the 'real I' assumes the form of whatever it gets associated with. Though water in essence is formless, when it occupies a glass, it becomes the glass, as it were; upon occupying a jug, it becomes the jug, as it were. By being associated with the world, 'I' became the world. In essence, the whole world is a marvellous expression of 'I'. Due to association with every body, the 'I' tends to identify with the individual forms, thereby leading to the perception of diverse individuals. Diversity was only meant to be an aspect of God's expression (of 'I'). However, everywhere, there has been an innate tendency to forget the primary purpose.

He, who has attained the experience of God, can effortlessly communicate the nature of that experience in various ways. He need not put in effort to think about it; he need not refer to scriptures to describe it. He verbalises whatever happens perpetually, at every moment of time. If a discourse in an auditorium is just meant to tell how many columns are there in the auditorium or how many lamps or what is the size of the audience, it can be very easily counted and told, as one only needs to talk about what one beholds before him. As these things are visible and tangible, they can be easily explained. However, we are discussing the experience which is invisible. For one who realises the self, conveying that experience in words becomes as simple as describing the items in the auditorium. After self-realisation, the experience, which is invisible, imperceptible, intangible for everyone, becomes easily visible to him.

When the secret is revealed, everything becomes simple

There were saints who were illiterate, who did not belong to any aristocratic family, nor were they born into higher castes. Some saints belonged to the (traditionally regarded as) lowest castes and had no formal education; yet the words of truth that they expressed were such that even the most erudite scholars were astounded. People wondered how such profound words of wisdom could emerge from these saints; words that we cannot even think of with our rational intellect. What indeed was the understanding that these saints had gained? That secret is now gradually unfolding before you.

Some examples are provided throughout the book in order to make it possible for the seeker to understand the truth. Every person addresses himself as 'I'. This means that basically everyone's name is 'I'. Whenever any person talks to himself or about himself, he says, "I do this, I do that, I went, I came..." He addresses others by using the names they are known with. He does this so that he can recognise and distinguish between them. Else, if he were to use the word 'I' to refer to everyone, then everyone would have been known by the same name. Therefore, people are given different names for the sake of convenience.

Government records demand that names should be able to address people individually. If everyone was to furnish the name 'I' for government records, it would not work. Thus names are given for the sake of convenience. If names are only meant for convenience, then it would not matter what name is assigned to you. If you are asked to perform a role on the stage and given some name, you would say, "That's perfectly fine. No problem." Whether it is this name or that, it does not matter. You will not be worried as it would serve as only a label given to you so that others can identify you. Now, if you are supposed to perform a role, why not perform it thoroughly and give your best; why do it by feeling miserable? By adopting this attitude, everything changes. Even if you are supposed to perform the act of crying, you will play it to perfection. If your act of crying were to help someone emerge out of grief, you would cry with all your intensity. Even crying would then be the expression of your self.

Let 'I' be attached to the 'real I'

You would have understood the fifth secret, wherein you saw that when the 'I' got associated with glass, it became glass. Likewise, when the 'I' got associated with the body, it became the body. When 'I' got associated with intellect, it became intellect. When 'I' got associated with the mind, it became the mind. When this very 'I' gets attached with the 'real I', it becomes God. You need to decide what 'I' should be associated with. If you do not associate 'I' with anything, it will attach itself to something. 'I' can never sit still.

In the case of some people, 'I' gets attached to their position or designation. They get identified with their position and become reluctant to leave it. If their position is snatched away from them, they feel as if "I am dead". In case of some others, 'I' gets attached to some other body (person). When that other person dies, they commit suicide, thinking, 'What is the use of living now?' All this has been happening in ignorance till today. If the 'I' is not attached to the 'real I', what does it do? In ignorance, it gets attached to anything at all. The 'I' never realises as to what it is getting attached to. And whatever it gets attached to, the 'I' assumes it to be itself.

Let the 'I' unite with the 'real I'; let it only perform a role with everything else. When it gets associated with the body, let it only perform the role of the body; let it not get truly attached to the body. Let it get attached to the body only to the extent that is necessary to protect the body. If the 'I' gets attached to the body indiscriminately, it becomes the cause of suffering. If the body is injured, dress up the wound. If your hand accidentally touches fire, move your hand away. At that time do not say, 'Since I am not the body, it does not matter even if the hand is burnt.' Always use your commonsense together with knowledge.

When the 'I' gets associated with the 'real I', it is formless

When the 'I' gets associated with the 'real I', it becomes formless. When water occupies a jug or a glass, it assumes a shape. However, when water merges into the ocean, it becomes formless. You say, "This is a glass of water; this is a jug of water." However, you never say, "This is an ocean of water." This is because water loses its form in the ocean. There, only the ocean exists. Now, you must have understood what the 'I' ought to be associated with.

Due to association of the 'I' with the body, man thinks, "If I am going through misery, others should also suffer." By thinking this way, he engages himself in causing pain and agony to others. This is what happens in ignorance. To avoid this, the 'I' needs to be trained to associate with the 'real I'. This is the role of the spiritual master; he constantly reminds you and alerts you to stay associated with the 'real I'. This is because when you are associated with the 'real I', you realise that all the 'I's' (all people and all beings) of the universe are *you*. You would thereby never think of harming others.

You are not the words that you use to address yourself. You say, "Mine, me... my party's flag is yellow, which is dirty ..." When you say 'my party', it implies that you are not the party. 'My party's flag' implies that you are not the flag. If the flag is yellow, it implies that you are not yellow. 'Yellow, which is dirty' implies that you are not dirty. In reality, you are neither yellow nor dirty; you are neither the flag nor the party. In reality, you are the witness, the observer of all these.

As the number of labels (words) increase, the truth gets increasingly veiled. All these labels, such as 'my party', 'my party's flag', 'my flag's colour' take you away from the 'real I'. As these labels go on reducing, the 'I' will automatically begin to draw closer towards the 'real I' and eventually merge with it. Man tends to be focused outwardly, due to which, in the external world, he can easily grasp any missing link. However, he cannot grasp the missing link pertaining to his inner world. Let this missing link (secret) of the inner world help man progress in the inward journey.

When the 'I' gets associated with the 'real I', it becomes formless and unlimited.

Chapter Four

Definition of the 'Real I'

Who is the Body and Who am I?

If someone were to ask you, "Are you ready to set aside an hour a week for yourself?", you may reply, "I am already giving an hour of my time to myself. I watch television, I visit the garden, and I dine out in the restaurant with my family." Having said this, you may feel that you have set aside time for yourself; however, in reality you have not utilised that time for yourself. Even if you spend your entire day in front of the television, you have not given this time to yourself.

Instead, you have spent your time to satisfy your senses with whom you have identified yourself and consider them to be 'I'. When you identify yourself with your body, you would like your eyes to see beautiful scenery, your ears to hear melodious music, your nose to smell good perfume, and your tongue to taste delicacies. You spend your entire life fulfilling your sensual desires.

Here you identify yourself with your body, though you are not the body; rather the body is your companion, your friend. You are that experience of being, which transcends the body. You feel that you are the body, the mind, the intellect; but you are none of these. Your true nature is beyond these three. When you say, "My pen, my shirt," you are aware that the pen and the shirt are different from the one who possesses them (you). However, when you say, "My body," you are under the illusion that you are the body. Isn't this strange because you are not the body in reality! You are the one who says 'my'. How much time do you devote for this 'real I'? It is the time you give to the 'real I' that will truly satisfy you and bring fulfilment in your life. This time is meant for listening to the truth, service of the truth and devotion to God.

See it from the perspective of an author

People are going in different directions depending on their understanding and levels of awareness. They take decisions based on their wisdom and level of consciousness. If they realise that they have to travel in the same direction, they will try to align with each other, i.e. they will try to come on the same platform. It is only then that the truth, which is universal and the very substratum of all, will emerge. If all are not on the same platform (same level of consciousness), then the common underlying principle will not be visible. It is crucial to see this truth.

Different words are written on a paper using different colours like red, black, green and blue; however the background of all these words is the same paper. Let us understand this with another example. The following text is written on a piece of paper: 'There paper was paper a paper poet paper. One paper day paper he paper decided paper to paper write paper a paper poem paper. He paper picked paper up paper a paper paper paper.' When you read these lines, you do not understand their meaning. These are different words written with the word 'paper' in between each of them. When you read again by removing the word 'paper', you will understand the meaning, which is: 'There was a poet. One day he decided to write a poem. He picked up a paper.' In reality, what is it that exists in the space between two words? What is there in the gaps between the words? What are these words supported (written) on? When you read the newspaper, has it ever occurred to you to find what are these words kept on? How would these words exist without the paper?

'Words' here represent the human bodies. Just like words in diverse colours, there are diverse bodies. All the differences (conflicts) occur between these words (bodies) because they seem to be separate; their colours, forms and meanings are different. You meet many people — they all appear to have different purposes and goals; however, you are unable to comprehend the underlying universal principle which is the same in each of them. The reality is that the different colours, forms and purposes are also the same; they just appear to be different. They exist on the same paper. Without the paper, these words would not exist. What has to be understood is that the paper not only exists between these words but also behind them, and the word 'paper' was written between these words to serve as a reminder of the actual paper.

The word 'paper' is not the real paper but it reminds us of real paper. Why do you chant *mantras*? What is the purpose behind it? *Mantras* by themselves are not knowledge; the word 'silence' is not the real 'silence'. You have seen that the word 'paper' is written between words so as to remind the poet when he picks up the paper to write a poem that this is the very paper that exists between as well as behind the words and is the common underlying basis. It is one; it does not change when something is written on it. Words can be seen only because of it; therefore, its existence is essential. To unearth and grasp this secret through experience is real spirituality. You ought to experience this truth within you.

The body represents a 'word'. And how do you perceive the other words? How do you perceive the words, which are towards your left, right or in front of you? "If it is black, then I need to keep away from it; if it is beautiful, then I want to go close to it... This is white, this is good, that is bad..." However, now you will notice that all these words refer to *one* context to convey the story of the same poet (God). All the words express the same reality as there is only one story. There is no other story written on this paper of the world, and the same story of the world is going on since the beginning. When you realise that all the words come about only to keep the story going, then you experience bliss.

You may feel that the story has been stretched far too long; however, if you look at it from the author's point of view, he will say,

"This is just the beginning of the story. A lot of interesting episodes are yet to occur. A new twist, a U-turn, will take place in this story. A lot is yet to happen." However, you may tend to feel as though 2,007 years ago Jesus had come or 2,500 years ago the Buddha had come; thus many years have passed. The author says, "The story has just started; there is a variety of self-expression happening and has yet to happen. Different ways of expression emerged through the bodies of great saints like Mira, Kabir, Chaitanya Mahaprabhu, Ramkrishna Paramhansa, Raman Maharshi, Jesus, Prophet Mohammad, etc. A lot of expression is yet to happen. It is just the beginning and the climax is further ahead." To learn this art of seeing from the author's perspective, you will first need to surrender yourself to the truth and realise the truth.

Self-remembrance

To start with, self-remembrance or remembering your essential nature is essential to be understood. In order to understand this in depth, read the following example. A person says four lines about himself. From these four lines, one can understand how man says different things, assuming himself to be the body, mind, intellect and self (self-witness). You will understand how to use the words 'I', 'my', 'mine' in different contexts every time. Once you use the word 'I' to refer to the body, the other time you use the word 'I' to refer to the mind. Following are those four sentences:

- I went to the terrace.
- My hand got wounded.
- I felt bad.
- I thought of going to the doctor.

In the first case, when it is said, "I went to the terrace," the word 'I' is used to refer to the body. Likewise, you say many things during the day, referring to yourself as the body, e.g. I had food, I drank water, I went, I came, I laughed, I cried, etc. In all these examples, you speak with the assumption that you are the body. Here 'I' refers to the body.

In the second case, when it is said, "My hand was wounded," then who does 'my' refer to? Does it refer to the body? If you use the word 'I' to refer to the body, you would not say 'my hand'. When you say, "My hand was wounded," you consider yourself as being separate from your body. It is only when you consider yourself to be distinct from the body that you can say 'my hand'. Whenever you say, "My shirt, my pen," you are distinct from these objects. Similarly when you say, "my hand," it becomes clear that the hand is distinct from the one who uses the word "my". When you say "my body", it means that you are separate from the body; otherwise who is the one saying "my"? How can the body say "my body"? If you are John, do you say "my John"? Thus, it is experienced that there is someone who is apart from the body and who says, "My body is injured". This is the 'real I', the self.

In the third case, when you say, "I felt bad," you assumed yourself to be the mind. Your body cannot feel bad. Only your mind can feel bad. Therefore when you say, "I felt bad" or "I felt good," you assume yourself to be the mind.

In the fourth case, it is said, "I thought of going to the doctor". When the word 'thought' or 'thinking' is used, it means that intellect is being spoken about. Here you assume yourself to be the intellect.

Thus, in the same incident, at one instance, 'I' is assumed to be the 'body', in another instance, it is assumed to be the 'mind', the 'intellect', in yet another context, and in one instance the 'I' refers to the 'real I' which is underlying the body, mind and intellect.

In this example, only four sentences were quoted, wherein four different identities of 'I' could be understood. Upon deeper contemplation, you will come across different identities (superimpositions) of 'I'. Different identities of 'I' crop up at different points of time; but out of delusion, we always believe that the same 'I' is speaking. Actually, we should be using the word 'we' instead of 'I'. We ought to be saying, "we will go", "we felt" and so on because we have many identities of 'I' which go together. Once one 'I' raises its head and another at some other time. Being lost in the delusion of these several false identities of 'I', the 'real I' gets forgotten. The 'real I' says, "I never get the opportunity to come to the fore as the false 'I's keep coming in front. How do I emerge forth?"

Knowing the 'real I' through experience is the meaning of self-realisation. Understanding the 'real I' is very simple and yet very difficult. It is difficult because the 'real I' is too close to you. It is so close that you have never perceived it from that point of view. You make use of the four lines specified earlier a number of times, but you seldom remember the fact that each time you assumed yourself to be something different — either the body, mind or intellect.

This is self-remembrance — remembering your 'real I'. During the course of the day, whenever you remember this, ask yourself, 'When I use the words 'I', 'my', 'mine', then who is this 'I' I am referring to?' This will lead to elevation of consciousness.

Understanding the body

Lord Buddha understood the body in essence by working on his own body. He contemplated deeply on how the human body was formed. He realised that it is composed of countless atoms, molecules and experiences of various events. The human body consists of sixty trillion cells, where each cell contains a nucleus. The nucleus is 1,000 times smaller than the cell. Just visualise how small the nucleus must be! The cell itself is so small and the nucleus is 1,000 times smaller than the cell! There are protons and neutrons inside the nucleus and electrons revolving around the nucleus. Electrons revolve at the speed of 500-600 miles per second.

When the fan rotates, you never thrust your finger in between the blades of the fan, even though you are aware of the gap in the blades. Due to the high speed, you cannot find the gap and hence you do not insert your finger. Similarly in the human body there is a lot of empty space. If one thinks of thrusting a finger in the body, the finger could easily go in. However, this does not happen because the electrons are moving at a very high speed. This is what the Buddha realised through his experience. Today, science has also discovered the same with the help of modern gadgets.

The Buddha worked on his body and realised that electrons are of varied nature. Their nature is regulated by different principles such as fire, air, water and Earth. Whenever you sweat, the water principle surfaces on the skin. The Buddha realised the different vibrations in the body but the 'real I' lay beyond that.

Just because the Buddha started his search for the truth from the body, it does not mean that everybody should follow the same. One can straightaway start from the 'self', the 'real I', thinking that one should understand the self first. One can also start with the mind. The ultimate goal is to attain the 'self' — the 'real I'.

Get attached to the body only to the extent that is necessary to protect the body. If the 'I' gets attached to the body indiscriminately, it becomes the cause of suffering.

Chapter Five

The Body is Man's Companion

How to Implement the Fifth Secret in Your Life

From the fifth secret, you would have understood where man goes wrong. After gaining spiritual knowledge, some people say, "I am God"; however, they do not realise that this statement is incorrect. "I am not God; rather God is 'I'", is the correct statement. An individual can never be God. The 'I' which is present within everyone is one and the same; that 'real I' is God. If this is understood, then one will never be egoistical about possessing knowledge. Otherwise people live with the ego of their knowledge.

Let there be the conviction that God and 'I' were associated with each other due to language and for the purpose of self-experience. Let there be the conviction that the body is meant to be the means of expression of the real self. Then whenever you see anything transpiring in the body, you will never say, "This is happening with *me*." You would say, "All this is happening with my companion." Consider two people travelling together. One of them is your friend, your companion, your buddy, who knows everything about you, as he is like your shadow that follows you everywhere; how would you regard him? If something happens to this companion, you will never say that it has happened to you. When your friend says, "I am hungry," you will say, "My friend, my companion, is hungry." You will not experience the suffering that he is going through.

Just as you introduce your friend, "This is my companion," in the same way address your body thus: "This body is my companion." Consider your body as your companion. You are *with* your body, but you are not the body. When you feel hungry, say to yourself, "My companion is hungry." If there is pain in your body, say to yourself, "My companion is experiencing pain."

Whilst saying this, you need to make use of your commonsense. Do not neglect your companion (the body), as it is the medium for your expression. If your companion (body) is injured, you need to dress its wounds. But while doing so, do not get unduly attached to your body. For instance, if one of your relatives passes away, you will not say, "My relative passed away." Instead you would say, "My companion's (body's) relative has passed away," regardless of that relative was close or distant, uncle or aunt, grandfather or grandmother. By saying this, you will not suffer due to grief or attachment. Even if you do feel sorrow, it will not be as intense.

Death is intended to make you contemplate. Death is a great teacher; however, people tend to forget this. People do not learn what they ought to from death. When your awareness level is elevated, you start living the fifth secret of life by not getting over-attached to the trials and tribulations of life, such as the ailments or demise of your kith and kin. You get firmly established in the conviction that these incidents are happening with your companion, not with you.

From this conviction and faith will also arise the understanding that the companion (body) needs to be educated and trained so as to get prepared for the highest expression; it needs to be imbued with skills and expertise. The companion's capability and competence need to be enhanced as it always accompanies you. You will do whatever is required towards this end; however, it need not be a cause of concern for you. How do you feel when you resolve the problems faced by a friend of yours? You find it easy to solve his difficulties.

However, you find it difficult to solve your own problems. You keep worrying, 'How will it get resolved? When will it get resolved? When will I settle down in life? Will I get a job? When will I get it? Will I be able to enjoy the job?' But, henceforth you will say that all this is happening with your companion (body). Whether you use the word 'friend' or 'companion' or 'buddy', the essential understanding should be that you are not the body.

Nevertheless, it is practical to assume your identification with the body for the purpose of communicating with the external world. Whilst speaking to people, you would say, "I am in pain; I am suffering"; at the same time you will say to yourself, 'In reality, all this is happening with my constant companion!' Promptly tell yourself that whatever you said was only meant for people listening to you. While saying this to yourself, you need not feel that you are lying or deceiving people. Instead, you are saying it out of love; otherwise people who listen to you would be confused.

Five symbolic gestures (*mudras*) representing the five secrets

In the 'House of the Supreme', you were told about the five symbolic gestures (*mudras*). The gesture of the five fingers reminds you about the first secret. The five fingers indicate the five aspects of a problem, viz. solution, gift, ladder, lesson and challenge.

According to the second secret, you will focus on the present by making use of the single-handed clap (snap of the fingers).

The third secret covers four aspects — love, attention, money and time. You were told how to give these forms of wealth to others as well as to yourself.

The fourth secret is depicted by the bracket ( ) *mudra* using the thumb and index finger. In this secret, you were given the *mantra*, 'This is *that* what I need', which has to be used with commonsense. Do not misuse this *mantra* with a negative intent or to fuel your obsessions.

The fifth secret is epitomised by your body itself, regardless of its state. According to the fifth secret 'You are *with* the body; you are not the body.'

You have understood the five secrets of life in conjunction with these *mudras*; what next?

Man has two births. The first birth is when he comes into this world and the second is when his ignorance is annihilated and the truth is revealed. This is known as self-realisation. This is man's second birth.

Chapter Six

How to Carry Your Companion Along

Experience the Joy of Associating with the Body

We already know from experience what happens if we water agarden to provide water to each and every flower, each and every leaf, but neglect the roots. We know we should water the roots first. But your mind may ask, 'There is "nothing" at the roots — no leaves, flowers or fruits; then why should I water the roots?' You will have to tell it, 'That "nothing" in essence is everything. Water has to be given to the roots.'

Your root is the self. Are you paying attention to your self, your true nature of being? Are you doing something for that? You are doing everything for what you are not and neglecting what you actually are. Self-realisation reminds you to attend to that 'nothingness' which is your essential being, the 'real I'. Contemplate whether all the effort you put in is for your essential being or for what you are not (the body).

After self-realisation, all anger, malice and other negative aspects in an individual come to an end as he realises that he is not the body; his notions pertaining to the body (fear of death, other fears, worry, jealousy, hatred, etc.) dissolve. The fear of death is the basic fear underlying all the fears of an individual. The fear of death implies the fear of death of the body. This fear also disappears after self-realisation (after knowing the essential nature of being — the 'real I').

Example of a porter

When a porter carries luggage, his constant focus is to reach as soon as possible the designated spot where he has to offload the luggage. Likewise, after realising the truth (self-realisation), man carries his body around with the attitude that one day he will cast off his body. It could be sixty or even eighty years away. After self-realisation, man is able to relate to the body in this manner with such ease. Will he then be delighted or miserable when he has to leave the body? He will experience only bliss when he has to abandon the body. However, the difference between a porter and the one who is self-realised is that the self-realised does not consider the body as a burden.

A weightlifter practises lifting of weights. While he too lifts weights just like a porter, he does not consider it a burden. He is only happy to increase the weights that he lifts. Similarly, after self-realisation, man experiences bliss even while carrying the body around; he does not consider the body as a burden. At the same time, he is not attached to the body and can easily cast it away when the time comes. A common man gets attached to the body and is afraid of losing it. After realising the truth, man does not have any qualms in discarding the body at the time of death.

In this way, man undergoes considerable inner transformation after self-realisation, without any visible change in his external behaviour. Conversely, it is also possible that the external behaviour may change after self-realisation. Do not assume that there would be no external changes at all. After self-realisation, some people speak while others prefer to remain silent. Mira started dancing after self-realisation; the Buddha remained in meditation. After self-realisation, the external expressions of different people vary. Therefore, do not be under the notion that whatever happens with a given self-realised person will happen with others too.

You are doing everything for what you are not and neglecting what you actually are.

Chapter Seven

How to Realise the Self

Attain the True Purpose of Your Life

In the fifth secret you have understood that you are not the body. Finally, you need to understand who you are. At this step, you have to enquire into the true nature of your being. It is through this enquiry that you will realise your true self. How to enquire into yourself and what does this mean? Let us understand this through the following example.

A person is standing beside water and his reflection is seen in the water. As there are ripples in the water, his reflection seems to move; then will he be sad, thinking, 'I am moving?' No. This is because he knows, 'this is my reflection; it's not me. If my reflection is moving, it does not mean that I am moving.' Similarly, contemplate on *who* is getting affected by unhappiness? *Who* is unhappy? Is your companion (body-mind mechanism) unhappy or are you? If you enquire within, you will find that you are unaffected; it is not *you* (the true you) who is unhappy, although you say, "Today I am very unhappy or anxious or disappointed or happy..." When you enquire within and reflect on your true nature, you will realise the fifth secret of life. Otherwise, you will live in delusion throughout your life. Let us understand self-enquiry in some detail.

Who I am not

You may begin self-enquiry by first asking, 'Who I am not?' The answers you may get are:

- I am not this body because the moment I say that this is my body, then it is something external; not me. Just as I am not 'my car'.
- The name given to this body is not me.
- The five elements of this gross body — earth, fire, water, air and ether are not me.
- The astral body within this body is not me.
- The five senses of the body — eyes, ears, nose, tongue, and skin are not me.
- I am not those things that are related to the senses — sight, sound, smell, taste or touch.
- I am also not the breath due to which this 'body-mind' mechanism functions.
- Neither am I the mind that thinks about what I should be.
- Nor am I the intellect that is absent along with the body during deep sleep.

Then, who are you? You are the only one who remains. It is you who is using the body and the five senses. It was you who is the master of the intellect. Now it is you who is the witness of the mind.

You are beyond every label. Now, if you no longer are the body, mind or intellect, then:

- How can you be an engineer or a doctor or a leader or a student?
- How can you be a brother or a sister, a father, a mother, a friend, a husband, a wife, a disciple or a guru?
- How can you be an American, Indian, British or Chinese?
- How can you be a Hindu, a Muslim, a Christian or a Jew?
- How can you be cheerful, intelligent, foolish, positive, active, honest, pious or lazy?

Who am I?

Now it is just you who remains — pure, non-state, without any imagination of name or form. Accept your true form as it is. And remain that. You have become something that you are not. Now it is time to be re-established in your consciousness, to be who you actually are.

Words cannot express the nature of self. But its nature has been described as *sat-chit-anand. Anand* means 'bliss'. *Sat* signifies the truth, which is the silence (maun) behind the mind. *Chit* signifies the mind. The truth (*sat*) created the mind and then identified itself with the mind and thus the individual was created and then bliss (*anand*) manifested. This is not possible in any other being on Earth, but man.

If you remain at that place where thoughts arise, then you will realise the self. 'I' thought is the first thought. That is why if one enquires, 'Who am I?' continuously or devotes some time every day to ask himself this question in solitude, the answer is bound to come. Answer, not from the intellect, but by actually being there. This question is the 'root question', the first question. Assuming that this 'I' thought has a body, then its 'feet' are rooted in the witness, the self, and other thoughts arise from its 'head'. Till the 'I' thought does not arise, other thoughts cannot arise. Go to the root of thoughts and a 'thoughtless state' will manifest.

Attaining the thoughtless state

Mind means thoughts. Being thoughtless means being in a 'no-mind' state. To quieten the mind, self-enquiry is the most beautiful method. This method is the path (means) as well as the destination (end). When you ask, 'Who am I?', then this thought in the form of a question will end all other thoughts. While this enquiry is on, other thoughts cannot remain. After ending all other thoughts, this last thought of 'Who am I?' will also end itself. Then self-realisation takes place. This will break the concept of form or the body. You are not limited by the body. You are unlimited. You will come to know this by experience. That is why self-enquiry is the most effective method to make the mind thoughtless.

However advanced a meditator may be, thoughts continue to crowd the mind. We need a very potent thought to annihilate these thoughts; a thought that will annihilate all the thoughts. You need a diamond to cut a diamond. An antidote for a poison is another poison.

In the same way, let one thought annihilate all other thoughts. 'Who am I?' is one such thought which will end every thought, notion, belief and concept. All we need is to learn how to use this potent weapon.

Whenever a thought appears — be it of fear, greed, rejection, worry, etc. — ask yourself, 'To whom has this thought occurred?' Or ask, 'Who was afraid?' or 'Who felt the rejection?' Then the reply will emerge, 'To me'. Now ask, 'Who, me? Who am I?' Thus you will reach your centre (source) whenever this question arises, and for a few moments you will be immersed in the bright silence (*maun*) within you. In this silence, will arise the 'supreme truth' and you will realise the self. Another thought will appear after a few moments. You will again ask the question, 'To whom has this thought occurred?' This will cut the thought off and the reply will be 'To me.' Then again ask, 'Who is this me?'

Self-stabilisation and self-expression

You may begin this enquiry every day for twenty minutes, and very soon you will be able to continue this enquiry throughout the day even while working and you will know the reply through your own experience. In this way, the 'Who am I?' thought will annihilate all other thoughts and will finally annihilate itself.

Continue this enquiry until you find out your true identity, till all your concepts about yourself dissolve — such as you are the body. The moment these concepts (beliefs) dissolve, self-enquiry will end because now you would have stabilised your self (*sthitapragnya*). After that, even if there are thoughts, you would have understood that these are not 'my' thoughts. They do not occur to me. I am the witness beyond these. Thoughts are in my body-mind mechanism. This machine is just a mirror which makes me aware of myself. If there are thoughts occurring in this mirror, how can they trouble me? The mirror always does its work. It always reveals my presence to me. It always makes me aware of my awareness. Practising self-enquiry and thus being established in oneself is the highest devotion of all. Eliminating thoughts the moment they arise by the process of self-enquiry is the truest sacrifice of all.

You can thus experience your true self or attain self-realisation through self-enquiry as well as through complete meditation described under the second supreme secret of life. With continuous practice, preferably under the guidance of a true spiritual master, you can attain the ultimate state of self-stabilisation followed by supreme self-expression arising out of pure bliss. In this way, the purpose for which you came to Earth will be fulfilled.

When the consciousness is asleep, the mind becomes the master. When consciousness declares Itself to be the master through self-knowledge, then the mind becomes the servant.

Glossary

Self

The Universal Self, the true self, consciousness, life, the formless, the self-witness, the Creator, God, Lord, Allah.

Samadhi

The state of consciousness before time began. *Samadhi* is a state, which cannot be adequately described in words; it can only be experienced. It can be said that *samadhi* is being conscious of the true self, transcending time and space, or being in the state of undifferentiated being — a state of complete calm, tranquillity and joy where the mind continues to be alert. A second meaning is to voluntarily enter the state of death, or conscious death, or arranged death.

Knowledge

In the entire book, it implies the knowledge related to truth.

Tej

Tej is one of the most important words coined by Sirshree. 'Bright' is the closest translation of this word. Let us understand *tej* or bright, with the help of examples. There is happiness as also unhappiness. Here happiness means the opposite of unhappiness. But there also exists happiness that is beyond both these polarities and is called *tej* happiness or bright happiness. This means that when the word *tej* or bright is used as an adjective, then the word that is described as 'bright' is beyond both the polarities.

Tejgyan

Tejgyan or 'bright knowledge' means knowledge beyond knowledge and ignorance. It is the knowledge of the final truth.

Tejguru

Spiritual master who guides you towards attainment of the final truth and stabilisation in that truth.

Bright love

Supreme love, Divine love or bright love is unconditional, unquestioning, unlimited, unchanging, eternal and true love. It transcends all other love as also hatred. It is overflowing love for the Lord and all His creations. All conditions cease in supreme love, because love in itself is immense joy.

Bright faith

Faith, that is beyond faith and doubt. It is faith that remains unshaken in any situation, no matter what.

Maun

Maun signifies the state of inner silence, which is the intrinsic nature of our true self. It is the state beyond sound and silence, beyond speech and thought. Words appear from this inner silence and also disappear into it. There is silence between every word and behind every word. There is silence between every thought and behind every thought. On the paper of silence, the words of the thought are written. To attain that silence is to attain the self.

Contrast mind

This is a phrase used to distinguish between two distinctive types of functioning of the mind — the first is the simple/instinctive/intuitive mind, which is essential for our functioning; second is the 'contrast' mind which refers to the mind which compares and judges everything. It splits everything into two — white or black (good or bad), like the contrast control feature on the television. This is the mind which gives rise to fear, worry, envy, insecurity, deceit, assumption, anger — in fact, it is the root cause of all our miseries in life. It is the one cause which hinders us from seeing the truth.

Tejasthan

Tejasthan literally means the 'bright place', the place where the self is connected with the body; where the formless and the form unite; where the *yog* (union) takes place. It can also be called as our source or centre, which is roughly estimated to be in the area of the heart.

Bright *knowlerience*

'*Knowlerience*' is a new word coined by the Tej Gyan Foundation and refers to spiritual knowledge gained from inner experience.

Maya

This whole world is *maya* created by the self. *Maya* is generally regarded as an illusion. However, there is a subtle distinction between the nature of *maya* versus illusion. *Illusion* refers to something that doesn't exist; *maya*, on the other hand, is existent and non-existent at the same time, like a dream. The experience you have seems absolutely real so long as you are seeing the dream. Therefore, the *maya* of the dream cannot be called non-existent. Yet, when awake, one realises that the dream was an illusion, a false world.

Self-expression

Expression of the true Universal Self.

Self-meditation

Meditation on the true Universal Self.

Temple

A place of worship, which could be a temple, a church, or a mosque.